EMBRACING BRILLIANCE

NURTURING YOUR INNER LIGHT

DR. OSCAR HARRIS

Foreword

Welcome to the illuminating journey, "Embracing Brilliance: Nurturing Your Inner Light," authored by Dr. Oscar Harris. Within the confines of these pages lies a roadmap to self-discovery, authenticity, and purpose—a guide crafted to help you uncover the radiant brilliance that resides within you.

In a world where the clamor of daily life often drowns out the whispers of our true selves, Dr. Harris offers a beacon of hope and clarity. With wisdom gleaned from years of experience in psychology, personal development, and spiritual growth, he invites you to explore your inner landscape deeply.

Through the pages of this book, Dr. Harris provides practical tools, insightful exercises, and heartfelt anecdotes to aid you in your quest for self-understanding and fulfillment. From identifying your core values to setting meaningful goals and living authentically, each chapter is a stepping stone to embracing your unique brilliance.

But more than just a guide, "Embracing Brilliance" is a testament to human potential's power and individuality's beauty. Dr. Harris reminds us that within each of us lies a spark of divinity, waiting to be fanned into a flame of purpose and passion.

As you journey through these pages, may you be inspired to embrace the fullness of who you are—to honor your gifts, acknowledge your strengths, and shine your light brightly upon the world? May you discover that true brilliance is not found in pursuing external validation or material success but in the quiet moments of self-reflection and inner knowing.

Dr. Oscar Harris has dedicated his life to helping others unlock their potential and live lives of meaning and fulfillment. In "Embracing Brilliance," he shares his insights, wisdom, and compassion with all who seek to awaken their inner light.

So, dear reader, I invite you to open your heart and mind to the transformative journey within these pages. May you walk this path with courage, curiosity, and an unwavering belief in your brilliance.

Warm regards,

HARRIS

TABLE OF CONTENTS

EMBRACING THE POWER OF LOVE AND SERVICE 110

CHAPTER 1

DISCOVERING YOUR INNER BRILLIANCE

"Everything you can imagine is real."

- Pablo Picasso

Understanding the complexity and depth of one's brilliance is paramount in the journey to self-discovery and personal growth. Brilliance, in its essence, is not a singular attribute but a composite of various dimensions that make an individual truly stand out. This exploration into the multifaceted aspects of personal brilliance invites one to embark on a profound journey of understanding, recognizing, and ultimately embracing the diverse layers that contribute to one's unique shine.

The first layer of brilliance can be found in an individual's innate talents and strengths. These natural abilities come effortlessly, whether in artistic expression, analytical thinking, or empathetic understanding of others. Through the recognition and cultivation of these innate gifts, one begins to tap into one's potential for greatness. However, brilliance extends beyond what is inborn, reaching into the skills and knowledge acquired over time. Education, training, and life experiences all shape an individual's abilities, offering new dimensions of expertise and insight.

One's values and beliefs characterize another critical layer of brilliance. These foundational principles guide decision-making, influence behavior, and define what an individual stands for. A person's commitment to honesty, integrity, compassion, or perseverance illuminates their character, showcasing brilliance in navigating life's complexities and interacting with the world around them.

An additional layer of personal genius is emotional intelligence, the ability to recognize, manage, and express one's emotions and manage interpersonal interactions sensibly and sympathetically. To succeed and form deep relationships, it is essential to have the capacity to comprehend, control, and affect one's own emotions as well as those of others. This aspect of brilliance is often overlooked, yet it is vital in fostering resilience, adaptability, and genuine relationships.

Furthermore, personal brilliance shines through an individual's passions and interests. The pursuits that ignite a fire within, whether creative endeavors, intellectual quests, or advocacy for a cause, reflect one's true essence and bring a sense of purpose and fulfillment. In pursuing these passions, one finds joy, inspiration, and the drive to make a significant impact.

Lastly, how an individual faces challenges and overcomes obstacles reveals an invaluable layer of brilliance. Resilience is the strength, bravery, and tenacity that allows one to overcome adversity and keep going on. The experiences gleaned from facing hardships contribute to personal growth and enrich one's perspective, making resilience a key component of brilliance.

Personal brilliance is not a monolithic trait but a complex amalgamation of talents, knowledge, values, emotional intelligence, passions, and resilience. Recognizing and embracing these layers within oneself paves the way for a life of achievement, fulfillment, and contribution. Through this holistic understanding of personal brilliance, individuals can truly shine, offering their unique light to the world. The journey to uncover and nurture these multifaceted aspects of brilliance is challenging and rewarding, inviting each person to discover the depth and breadth of their potential.

The Role of Curiosity in Unveiling Potential

Curiosity is vital in unlocking the door to one's full capabilities. The spark leads to discovering new skills, talents, and areas of interest that one might not have realized they possessed. Encouraging exploration and curiosity is essential in personal growth and self-discovery. It nudges individuals to venture beyond their comfort zones, ask questions, and seek new experiences, thereby unveiling layers of potential that lie dormant.

The desire to learn and understand more about the world and oneself is at the heart of curiosity. This eagerness to explore is not just about acquiring new information but deepening one's understanding and connection with various aspects of life. When channeling curiosity effectively leads to a fulfilling quest for knowledge and self-improvement. It encourages individuals to experiment, to try new things, and to learn through the process, regardless of the outcome.

Exploration driven by curiosity can take many forms. It could be as simple as picking up a new hobby, enrolling in a course to learn something unrelated to one's current profession, or even engaging in conversations with people from diverse backgrounds and walks of life. Each action is a step towards discovering one's hidden talents and strengths. For example, someone might find a passion for painting after attending an art class out of curiosity, or someone else might find they have a knack for public speaking by volunteering to lead a presentation.

Moreover, curiosity fosters problem-solving and critical thinking skills. When faced with challenges, a curious individual is likelier to explore various solutions, ask insightful questions, and think outside the box. This helps overcome the immediate challenge and builds a resilient and adaptive mindset that is invaluable in all areas of life.

To cultivate curiosity, it is important to create an environment that encourages questioning and open-mindedness. This involves embracing uncertainty and viewing it not as a hindrance but as an opportunity for growth and learning. It means not fearing the unknown but being excited by its possibilities. Celebrating small discoveries and achievements along the way also reinforces the value of curiosity and keeps the flame of exploration alive.

Encouraging exploration and curiosity requires a shift in perspective. One must view life as a continuous learning journey where every experience, whether success or failure, offers valuable lessons and insights. One must recognize that potential is not a fixed attribute but an evolving set of capabilities that can expand and deepen through curiosity-driven exploration.

Curiosity is not just a trait but a powerful tool that unlocks the door to discovering one's strengths and potential. A fulfilling journey of personal development and self-discovery can be started by encouraging awe and receptivity to new experiences. The role of curiosity in unveiling potential is unparalleled, as it propels individuals toward a life of continuous learning, exploration, and fulfillment.

Overcoming the Fear of Exploration

Facing new challenges and stepping into the unknown can be scary. It's natural to feel fear when considering exploring new areas of life, especially when discovering more about ourselves. However, overcoming these fears is a crucial step towards growth and self-discovery. Here are some strategies to help tackle these fears and embrace the journey of exploration.

Start Small: One way to ease into exploration is by taking small steps. Instead of diving headfirst into something completely unfamiliar, try starting with something closer to your comfort zone. Small victories and experiences can build your confidence, making it easier to take on more significant challenges later on.

Learn from Others: Hearing about other people's experiences can be incredibly inspiring. Talk to friends and family, or even look for stories online about people who have successfully navigated the path of self-discovery. Understanding the difficulties they encountered and how they overcame them can offer insightful knowledge and inspiration.

Focus on the Process, Not Just the Outcome: Sometimes, fear comes from worrying too much about the result. Instead, focus on the experience and what you can learn from it. Remember that every occasion offers valuable lessons, whether it leads to success or failure.

Mindfulness and Reflection: Practice being in the moment and reflecting on your feelings without judgment. Mindfulness can help you understand your fears better and approach them with a calmer mindset. It is critical to recognize that fear is a natural response but not let it control your actions.

Seek Support: You don't have to embark on the journey of exploration alone. Seek support from friends, family, or a mentor who can encourage you and provide advice. Sometimes, knowing that someone else believes in you can give you the courage to move forward.

Educate Yourself: Fear often comes from the unknown. By educating yourself about what you're interested in exploring, you can demystify it and reduce fear. Whether through books, online courses, or workshops, gaining knowledge can empower you to take the following steps.

Visualize Success: One effective method for conquering fear is visualization. Spend a few minutes daily closing your eyes and visualizing yourself accomplishing your objectives and conquering your worries. Engaging in this mental exercise can make you feel less anxious about the future and more confident.

Accept that Fear is Part of the Process: It's essential to accept that feeling scared is a natural part of trying new things. Instead of trying to eliminate fear, learn to move forward despite it. Recall that bravery is the will to act despite fear, not the absence of it.

Overcoming the fear of exploration is essential for personal growth and self-discovery. Applying these strategies allows you to navigate your fears and open yourself up to new experiences and opportunities. Each step you take, no matter how small, is a step towards understanding yourself better and unlocking your full potential.

The Power of Diverse Experiences

Life is a rich tapestry woven from the many threads of our experiences. Each new adventure, challenge, and encounter adds color and depth, shaping who we are and highlighting our unique brilliance. The variety of experiences one goes through plays a crucial role in uncovering and understanding one's true potential and talents. Let's delve into how embracing diverse backgrounds can illuminate the many facets of our brilliance.

Firstly, diverse experiences push us out of our comfort zones. In these moments, when we're a bit uncomfortable and unsure, we often discover strengths we didn't know we had. You must navigate a foreign city where you don't speak the language and realize you're more resourceful and adaptable than you thought. Or a new hobby challenges you unexpectedly, revealing patience and determination you hadn't had the chance to exercise before. These situations show us parts of ourselves waiting to be discovered.

Secondly, engaging in a variety of experiences broadens our perspective. It's easy to get stuck in a bubble, seeing the world only through the lens of our routine and familiar surroundings. By stepping into different cultures, trying new activities, or changing our daily habits, we open ourselves up to new ways of thinking and seeing the world. This expanded viewpoint can spark creativity, inspire new ideas, and lead us to paths we might never have considered otherwise.

Moreover, varied experiences teach us resilience and flexibility. Life is unpredictable, and the more we expose ourselves to different situations, the better equipped we become to handle whatever comes our way. Every new experience offers the chance to overcome obstacles, adjust to unfamiliar surroundings, and maintain optimism and an open mind in uncertainty. These traits are extremely helpful in overcoming barriers and boldly pursuing our objectives in life.

Diverse experiences also enrich our empathy and understanding of others. By walking in different shoes, so to speak, we gain insights into lives and perspectives different from our own. This enhanced empathy makes us better listeners, friends, and collaborators. It helps us build deeper connections with those around us and fosters a sense of community and belonging. These relationships may lead to positive learning and development cycles by opening doors to fresh experiences and possibilities.

Finally, embracing various experiences allows us to find what lights us up. It's through trial and error that we discover our passions and interests. A random cooking class ignites a passion for culinary arts, or a volunteer opportunity reveals a deep desire to help others. These discoveries are clues to our core motivations and values, guiding us toward a more fulfilling and purpose-driven life.

The power of diverse experiences lies in their ability to reveal our hidden strengths, broaden our perspectives, teach us resilience, enrich our empathy, and guide us to our passions. Through proactively pursuing and accepting novel encounters, we enable ourselves to discover and comprehend the whole of our genius. So, challenge yourself to step out of the familiar, embrace the unknown, and let the diverse tapestry of experiences illuminate the unique glow within you.

Creating a Vision for Your Future Self

Crafting a vision for your future self is like drawing a map for an exciting journey ahead. It's about dreaming big, setting your sights on the horizon, and imagining all the incredible possibilities when fully embracing your inner brilliance. Let's dive into how creating a vivid vision for your future can guide you toward a purpose, joy, and fulfillment-filled life.

To start, picture your future self in your mind's eye. Think about who you want to be, the qualities you wish to embody, and the accomplishments you aspire to achieve. This isn't about setting strict goals or timelines; it's more about allowing your imagination to run free and envisioning the best version of yourself. You may see yourself as a confident leader, a creative innovator, or a compassionate advocate for change. You can imagine living a life rich with adventure, creativity, or deep connections with loved ones. Whatever it is, let these images and feelings guide you.

Next, consider what embracing your inner brilliance entirely looks like. Your inner brilliance is that unique spark within you—your talents, passions, and values that make you. Fully embracing it means not holding back, not dimming your light to fit in, and not letting fear stop you from pursuing what sets your soul on fire. It means showing up as your authentic self, aligning with your values, and using your gifts to make a positive impact. Picture how this version of you moves through the world, the energy they bring to their endeavors, and their influence on those around them.

Creating a vision for your future self also involves imagining how you navigate challenges and setbacks. It's easy to envision success and happiness, but actual growth comes from resilience and the ability to bounce back stronger than before. Imagine your future self facing obstacles with grace, learning from each experience, and using these lessons to move forward with wisdom and courage. This portion of your vision prompts you to remember that every obstacle you face presents a chance to reaffirm your dedication to your path and greatness.

Now, consider the steps you can take today to move closer to that vision. While the future might seem far off, each day is an opportunity to lay the groundwork for the life you want to lead. It could be as simple as dedicating time to your passions, nurturing positive relationships, or investing in your personal growth. Small, consistent actions add up over time, gradually shaping you into the person you aspire to be.

Lastly, hold onto your vision with an open heart and mind. Life is unpredictable, and your dreams and desires might evolve as you do. Embrace flexibility and allow your imagination to grow and change with you. The key is to keep your inner brilliance—the core of who you are—at the heart of your journey.

Creating a vision for your future self is a powerful exercise in hope, ambition, and self-discovery. It invites you to dream without limits, to recognize and embrace your unique talents, and to chart a course toward a fulfilling and purposeful life. So, take some time to dream big and imagine the endless possibilities that await when you fully embrace your inner brilliance. Your future self will thank you.

CHAPTER 2

CULTIVATING AUTHENTICITY AND PURPOSE

"To love oneself is the beginning of a lifelong romance."

- Oscar Wilde

Knowing your core values is like holding a compass on a vast journey. These values are your north stars, guiding you through life's decisions, big and small. They shape your thoughts, actions, and interactions with the world around you. Identifying these values isn't just about putting names to what you already believe; it's about digging deep and uncovering the principles that truly define you. Here's a straightforward guide to help you on this journey of discovery.

Reflect on Your Most Memorable Moments

Start by reflecting on your life's most impactful moments—the highs and lows. These are when your emotions are at their peak, whether joy, pride, sadness, or anger. Ask yourself what these moments had in common. Perhaps you felt happiest when helping others, suggesting a core value of compassion or service. Or maybe injustice deeply angers you, pointing to fairness or justice as a core value. This reflection can reveal patterns that highlight your fundamental beliefs.

Consider What Makes You Feel Most Yourself

Think about when you feel most like yourself. What are you doing? Who are you with? These scenarios can reveal a lot about what matters to you. Creativity might be a core value if you feel most "you" when you're in the middle of a creative project. When volunteering, service and community could be central to who you are. Identifying these moments can help you pinpoint the values that bring you fulfillment and purpose.

Identify Your Influences

The people and messages that resonate with you can also reflect your core values. Think about role models, authors, or public figures you admire. What qualities in them do you wish to emulate? It could be their integrity, work ethic, or how they treat others. Similarly, consider which societal messages or themes inspire you or make you want to take action. These influences can serve as mirrors, reflecting your values to you.

Imagine Your Ideal World

Another helpful exercise is to picture the world you'd like to live in. What values are most prominent in this vision? Is it a world where everyone is treated equally, highlighting equality as a core value? Or is it a world where creativity and innovation thrive, suggesting that these are important to you? This imagination exercise can help clarify the values you wish to see more of in your surroundings—and, by extension, in yourself.

Write Them Down and Prioritize

Once you've gone through these steps, list the values that have surfaced. You might end up with a long list, and that's okay. The next step is to prioritize them. Which values feel non-negotiable? Which ones do you consider nice-to-haves but not essential to your identity? Through this process, aim to identify your top five core values. These principles are the ones you want to guide your life, the ones you're unwilling to compromise on.

Identifying your core values is a profoundly personal and enlightening process. It requires time, honesty, and a willingness to delve into your experiences and aspirations. Remember, your core values may evolve as you grow and encounter new experiences, and that's perfectly natural. The important part is that you have guiding principles that help you navigate life with integrity, purpose, and fulfillment.

The Journey Towards Authentic Living: Advice on living according to your values

Living authentically means making choices that align with your core values and the principles you hold dear. It's about being true to yourself in your thoughts, actions, and interactions with the world. This journey isn't always easy, but it's gratifying. Here are some advice to help you live more authentically, according to your values.

Stay True to Your Core Values

First, keep your core values close. Think of them as your compass that guides you through life's many decisions. Before deciding, big or small, ask yourself if it aligns with your values. If it doesn't, it might be worth reconsidering. This practice ensures that your actions reflect what's truly important to you.

Set Boundaries Based on Your Values

Setting boundaries is crucial in living authentically. These boundaries inform others about what is acceptable and not based on your values. For instance, if you value family time, you might set a limit by not checking work emails during family meals. Clearly defining these boundaries helps you stay true to your values and shows others what you stand for.

Surround Yourself with Support

The people around you can significantly impact your journey towards authentic living. Surround yourself with individuals who respect and support your values. These people will encourage you when you're living true to your values and hold you accountable when you stray. Positive support makes it easier to navigate the challenges of living authentically.

Be Kind to Yourself

The path to authentic living is a journey, not a destination, and it's okay to make mistakes along the way. Be kind to yourself during this process. If you realize you've made a decision that doesn't align with your values, treat it as a learning opportunity rather than a failure. Self-compassion is a crucial component of authentic living.

Reflect Regularly

Regular reflection is essential. Take time to reassess your values and actions and whether they still align. Life experiences can sometimes shift our values, and that's perfectly normal. Reflection ensures that you are always in tune with your deepest self and living a life that reflects that understanding.

Take Action Aligned with Your Values

Finally, take actions that reinforce your values. If you value community, get involved in local organizations or initiatives. If creativity is essential to you, dedicate time to your creative pursuits. Actions speak louder than words, and living your values through your efforts is the essence of authentic living.

Living according to your values isn't just about making the right choices but creating a life that feels genuinely yours. It involves constant reflection, making tough decisions, and sometimes standing alone. But the peace and fulfillment that come from knowing you're living true to yourself are unparalleled. So, embrace your values, let them guide you, and step confidently toward authentic living.

Reevaluating Life Goals in Light of Authenticity

Setting goals is a powerful practice, but ensuring these goals truly reflect your authentic self is vital for lasting fulfillment. Life's hustle or societal pressures often lead us to chase ambitions that don't align with our core values. Reevaluating your life goals in light of your authenticity means checking if what you're striving for resonates with who you are and what truly matters to you. Here's how you can align your goals with your authentic self.

Reflect on Your Core Values

Start by revisiting your core values. What principles are non-negotiable in your life? Your goals should respect these values and, ideally, celebrate and embody them. For instance, if the family is a core value, a plan that demands excessive travel or overtime at work might need reassessment.

Assess Your Current Goals

Take a good look at your existing goals. Ask yourself why you chose each one. Was it for personal satisfaction, or were you influenced by others' expectations or societal norms? If any goals don't truly resonate with your authentic self, let them go or reshape them into something that does.

Imagine Your Ideal Day

Visualizing your ideal day can provide insights into what authentic goals look like for you. What activities are you doing? Who are you with? How do you feel? This exercise can help identify goals that bring genuine happiness and fulfillment, providing a more precise direction for your ambitions.

Prioritize Goals That Feel Right

Once you've identified goals that align with your authentic self, prioritize them. It's better to focus on a few meaningful goals rather than chasing numerous ambitions that don't honestly speak to you. This prioritization ensures your energy is spent on what genuinely matters to you.

Set Flexible Goals

Remember that authenticity involves growth and change. Your goals should be flexible enough to evolve as you do. Setting rigid goals can lead to frustration if they no longer align with your authentic self over time. Allow room for adjustment and be open to reevaluating your goals regularly.

Embrace the Journey

Achieving goals is rewarding, but the journey there is equally important. Embrace the experiences, growth, and lessons learned along the way. Authentic living is as much about the path as the destination. Your goals should reflect the achievements you aspire to and the person you wish to become in the process.

Seek Support

Sharing your authentic goals with trusted friends or mentors can provide additional motivation and support. Choose to communicate with individuals who respect and understand your values. Their encouragement can be invaluable as you pursue goals aligned with your true self.

Reevaluating your life goals in light of your authenticity ensures that your ambitions serve your success, happiness, and personal growth. It's about making conscious choices that reflect your true self, leading to a more fulfilling and purpose-driven life. As you align your goals with your authentic self, you open the door to achieving your goals and living in harmony with who you are.

Building Confidence in Your Authentic Path

In a world brimming with expectations and norms, staying true to your authentic self is an act of courage and a commitment to personal integrity. Living a genuine life might be difficult because of the tremendous pressure to conform to social norms. However, building confidence in your authentic path is both possible and deeply rewarding. Here's how to navigate societal pressures and embrace the beauty of your true self.

Acknowledge the Pressure

The first step is acknowledging the existence of societal pressures. Whether about career choices, lifestyle, or personal beliefs, society often dictates a specific path as the 'ideal.' Recognizing these pressures helps you understand that the dilemma between following your heart and conforming to societal expectations is a shared experience. This awareness is crucial in developing the resilience needed to pursue your path.

Understand Your Authentic Self

To stay true to yourself, you must first know who you are. Spend time reflecting on your values, passions, and what brings you genuine happiness. Understanding your authentic self also involves recognizing your strengths and areas for growth. This self-knowledge is a foundation for making decisions that align with your identity rather than being swayed by external opinions.

Cultivate Self-Confidence

Building self-confidence is essential in overcoming societal pressures. Confidence in your authentic self comes from acknowledging your worth and believing in your capabilities.

Celebrate your achievements, no matter how small, and remember the times you stayed true to yourself, and it paid off. Practicing self-compassion and speaking kindly to yourself also strengthens self-confidence, helping you navigate moments of doubt gracefully.

Set Boundaries

Putting limits in place is a great strategy to safeguard your proper course. This means learning to say no to things that don't align with your values and being selective about the influences you allow into your life. Boundaries also involve managing the expectations of others, making it clear that your choices are your own. While setting boundaries can be challenging, especially with close friends and family, it's essential for preserving your sense of self.

Seek Supportive Communities

Surround yourself with people who respect and support your authentic self. This could be friends who encourage your dreams, family members who understand your values, or communities with similar interests. Supportive relationships offer encouragement and validation, making it easier to withstand societal pressures. Remember, you're not alone in your desire to live authentically; others are walking a similar path.

Embrace Your Unique Journey

Every individual's path is unique, and comparing your journey to others is a surefire way to undermine your confidence. Embrace the uniqueness of your path and celebrate the diversity of experiences it brings. Living authentically means accepting the ups and downs, learning from each experience, and strengthening your convictions.

Be Prepared for Challenges

Choosing to live authentically in the face of societal pressures is challenging. Be prepared for misunderstandings, judgments, or even resistance from those around you. However, remember that the fulfillment and peace from being true to yourself far outweigh the temporary discomfort of facing opposition.

Building confidence in your authentic path is a journey of self-discovery, resilience, and growth. By staying true to yourself and navigating societal pressures with courage and self-assurance, you pave the way for a life that is fulfilling and a true reflection of who you are. Remember, the world benefits most from individuals who dare to embrace their authenticity and share their unique light with those around them.

Finding Purpose in Daily Activities

With everything going on in our everyday lives, it's simple to get caught up in the routine and cross things off our to-do lists without considering them. Yet, there's a profound opportunity hidden in the ordinary—a chance to infuse everyday actions with intention and purpose, transforming the mundane into something meaningful. Here's how to weave meaning into the fabric of your daily life, making every action count.

Start with Mindfulness

Mindfulness is the gateway to living with intention. It's about being fully present and engaged in the current moment, not lost in thoughts about the past or future. Practicing mindfulness can turn even the simplest tasks into purposeful actions. Whether washing dishes, sending emails, or walking to the store, please focus on the job, notice the details, and consider the value it adds to your life or others. This presence of mind turns routine activities into moments of connection and gratitude.

Align Actions with Values

To give your everyday activities meaning, ensure they align with your basic principles. Identify what truly matters to you—kindness, creativity, growth, or community—and look for ways to express these values in your everyday actions. For example, if kindness is a core value, simple acts like greeting your neighbors or expressing appreciation to colleagues can be meaningful expressions of this principle. Aligning your actions with your values adds purpose to your day and ensures that you live in harmony with your true self.

Set Daily Intentions

Setting intentions at the start of each day can transform how you approach your tasks and interactions. A choice isn't a goal to be achieved but a mindset or quality you wish to embody, such as patience, generosity, or courage. By setting an intention each morning, you give direction to your day, making conscious choices that reflect your desired mindset. This practice turns everyday activities into opportunities for personal growth and fulfillment.

Find Learning Opportunities

No matter how mundane, every task has something to teach us if we're open to learning. Approach your daily activities with curiosity and the question, "What can I learn from this?" Organizing your workspace teaches you the value of clarity, and cooking a meal highlights the importance of nourishment and creativity. Viewing everyday actions as learning opportunities infuses them with purpose and enriches your personal development journey.

Contribute to a Greater Good

Finding purpose in daily activities can also come from seeing how your actions contribute to the greater good. Recognize the impact of your big and small choices in the broader world. Recycling, supporting local businesses, or conserving energy are examples of how routine decisions can reflect a commitment to sustainability and community welfare. A strong feeling of purpose is added to daily living when you realize that your activities affect people and things outside your immediate surroundings.

Practice Gratitude

Finally, cultivating a habit of gratitude can imbue your daily activities with purpose. Take time to acknowledge and appreciate the opportunity to engage in each task and its contribution to your life. Expressing gratitude for the ability to work, the food on your table, or the home you clean fosters a deep sense of purpose and fulfillment, transforming ordinary moments into gifts.

Infusing everyday actions with intention and purpose is about recognizing the significance of the small things, aligning your actions with your values, and appreciating the opportunity to make a difference daily. By adopting these practices, you turn everyday life into a meaningful journey filled with opportunities for growth, connection, and contribution.

CHAPTER 3

"Silence is a source of great strength."

- Lao Tzu

In the ever-spinning wheel of life, where each day rushes into the next, the power of stillness and reflection emerges as a profound force. This chapter delves into the transformative impact of pausing, stepping back from the relentless pace of daily routines, and embracing the stillness that fosters growth, understanding, and rejuvenation. Lao Tzu's timeless wisdom reminds us that within the realms of silence and introspection lies an untapped reservoir of strength. Here, we explore how dedicating time to stillness and reflection can illuminate our path, clarify our thoughts, and deepen our connection with ourselves and the world around us.

Developing a Practice of Mindful Stillness

Finding quiet moments can seem like a rare treasure in a world that's always buzzing with activity. Yet, mindful stillness, the art of simply being in the moment without doing anything, is a powerful tool that can bring calm and clarity into our busy lives. Here's a gentle guide on how to weave this practice into your daily routines, inviting peace and mindfulness into your everyday.

Start with small moments. You don't need to carve out hours of your day to embrace stillness. Begin with just a few minutes. In the morning, before the day's hustle begins, take a moment to sit quietly. No phone, no plans, just you and the morning. Let your thoughts pass without engaging with them, focusing instead on the calm of your surroundings.

Make it a natural part of your day. Incorporate stillness into actions you're already doing. While drinking your morning coffee or tea, for instance, focus entirely on the experience. Take note of the flavor, scent, and temperature of the cup. It's about being present and permitting oneself to take a mental break even while working on a straightforward activity.

Create a 'stillness signal.' Pick a regular occurrence in your day—a particular time, or maybe when you see something specific, like a tree outside your window—as a reminder to pause for a moment of stillness. This signal prompts you to stop, breathe, and center yourself, even for a few seconds.

Embrace waiting. In our fast-paced world, waiting is often seen as wasted time. Whether it's in line at the store or waiting for a webpage to load, these moments can become opportunities for stillness. Instead of reaching for your phone to fill every spare moment, try standing or sitting in awareness, using these snippets of time to practice being present.

Reflect before bed. As your day draws close, take a few moments to sit in stillness. Reflect on your day, not by running through what you did or didn't do, but by simply allowing yourself to be. This practice can be a peaceful bookend to your day, helping you to let go of the day's stresses and prepare for restful sleep.

Cultivating a practice of mindful stillness doesn't require dramatic lifestyle changes or hours of meditation. It's about finding and embracing those small moments in your day to pause, breathe, and be. By integrating these pockets of stillness into your routine, you invite a sense of peace and mindfulness into your life, offering yourself a quiet respite amid the day's demands.

The Reflective Journaling Path

Journaling, the simple act of putting thoughts and feelings onto paper, is a powerful tool for self-discovery. More than just a way to record daily events, this practice offers profound insights into our inner world, helping us better understand ourselves. The reflective journaling path can illuminate patterns in our thoughts and behaviors, provide clarity in moments of confusion, and serve as a private space for personal expression.

One of journaling's main advantages is its capacity to increase self-awareness. Writing down your ideas and emotions on a regular basis helps you identify deeper emotional undercurrents and reoccurring themes that can go unnoticed in the daily grind. As a result of this increased awareness, you may make better decisions, as you will have a clearer understanding of your objectives and motives.

Journaling also provides a safe outlet for expressing emotions. Whether you're grappling with sadness, joy, frustration, or gratitude, the pages of a journal offer unconditional acceptance. This act of expression is cathartic, helping to release pent-up emotions and reducing stress. Moreover, seeing your feelings reflected in you can make them easier to understand and manage.

Developing thankfulness is another crucial advantage. You could cultivate a more optimistic view of life by expressing gratitude in your notebook. This shift towards appreciation can improve mental well-being, increase resilience, and enhance overall satisfaction with life.

Reflective journaling also encourages personal growth. You're invited to reflect on your experiences, mistakes, and successes as you write. This reflection can foster a growth mindset, where challenges are seen as opportunities for learning rather than obstacles. Over time, you'll find yourself more open to new experiences, more adaptable to change, and more forgiving of yourself and others.

Lastly, journaling can serve as a record of your journey. Looking back on past entries, you can see how far you've come, recognize the challenges you've overcome, and celebrate your growth. This historical perspective can be incredibly motivating, reminding you of your resilience and ability to navigate life's ups and downs.

Incorporating reflective journaling into your daily or weekly routine doesn't require a significant time commitment or special tools—just a notebook and a pen. The key is consistency and honesty. Permit oneself to write freely, without concern about style or grammar. You'll discover that this easy exercise eventually yields profound realizations and a better comprehension of your life's path.

Wisdom in Solitude

Solitude, often misunderstood as loneliness, is, in fact, a state of rich self-discovery and introspection. Unlike loneliness, which is marked by a sense of isolation and longing for company, solitude is a chosen state of being alone where one can reflect, recharge, and connect deeply with oneself. Embracing solitude offers numerous benefits, shedding light on its wisdom.

Firstly, solitude fosters self-awareness. In the silence of being alone, without distractions or the influence of others, you can hear your thoughts and feelings more clearly. This quiet allows you to understand your desires, fears, and joys, guiding you toward a deeper understanding of who you are and what you truly want from life.

Solitude also enhances creativity. Many artists, writers, and thinkers have found their most profound ideas in moments of solitude. In this space, the mind can wander, explore, and make unique connections between seemingly unrelated concepts. Without the noise of constant social interaction or media consumption, your creative faculties have the freedom to flourish.

Moreover, solitude strengthens mental health. The constant barrage of stimuli can be overwhelming in today's fast-paced world. A retreat from this may be found in privacy, creating a calm setting where the mind can unwind and decompress. Regular periods of solitude can reduce anxiety and depression, leading to a more balanced and content state of mind.

Embracing solitude also cultivates resilience. By spending time alone, you become comfortable with your own company, which is invaluable in navigating life's ups and downs. Solitude teaches you that you can face challenges without relying on the constant presence or approval of others, reinforcing your inner strength and independence.

Finally, solitude enriches relationships. Paradoxically, time spent alone can improve how you interact with others. By better understanding yourself, you're more capable of understanding others. Solitude allows you to reflect on your relationships, appreciate them more deeply, and return to them with renewed patience, empathy, and insight.

Incorporating solitude into your life doesn't require drastic changes. It can be as simple as dedicating a few moments each day to sit quietly, taking a solitary walk, or setting aside time each week for reflection without electronic devices. The key is to approach solitude not as a void to be filled but as a space for growth and self-discovery.

In embracing solitude, you unlock a deeper connection with yourself. You discover the wisdom of your thoughts and feelings, gain clarity on your path in life, and cultivate a sense of peace and contentment that enriches all aspects of your existence.

Creating Sacred Spaces for Reflection

Creating a sacred space for reflection is like setting up a personal sanctuary—a dedicated spot where you can pause, breathe, and contemplate. This physical space, infused with tranquility and intention, becomes a retreat from the bustle of everyday life, encouraging deep reflection and inner peace. Here's how you can design such a space in your environment, transforming a corner of your world into a haven for contemplation.

Choose a Quiet Corner

Choose a peaceful area of your house where there won't be many distractions to begin with. It doesn't need to be large—a small nook or an unused room part can work beautifully. The key is that this space feels separate from the areas associated with daily activities and stress. It should be where you can close the door, literally or metaphorically, on the outside world.

Make It Comfortable

Comfort is crucial in a reflection space. Add items that make the area inviting and peaceful for you. This could be a comfortable chair or cushion, a soft throw blanket, or even a tiny mattress. The idea is to create a space where your body can relax, as physical comfort can significantly enhance your ability to engage in deep thought or meditation.

Incorporate Natural Elements

Incorporating natural elements into your environment might improve its peacefulness. Consider adding a small plant, a vase of fresh flowers, or even a bowl of stones or shells. Natural light is also a powerful element—choose a spot near a window if possible. These touches of nature can help ground you and foster a connection to the wider world, even as you turn inward.

Personalize with Meaningful Items

Personalize your space with items that hold special meaning for you. This could be photographs of loved ones, cherished keepsakes, inspirational quotes, or symbols of your faith or spiritual journey. These items serve as visual reminders of your values and aspirations, deepening your sacred space's sense of purpose and intention.

Keep It Uncluttered

Clutter can be distracting and counterproductive to reflection. Aim for a minimalist setup, keeping only those items that contribute to your sense of peace and purpose. An uncluttered space promotes a clear mind, making it easier to focus on your thoughts and feelings without external distractions.

Consider Aromatherapy

Scents can profoundly impact our mood and mindset. Consider incorporating aromatherapy into your sacred space through candles, incense, or essential oil diffusers. Scents like lavender, sandalwood, or jasmine can be soothing and conducive to a reflective mind.

Add Soft Lighting

Lighting is crucial when establishing an atmosphere. Soft, warm lighting can make your reflection space feel cozy and welcoming. You might use candles, fairy lights, or a lamp with a dimmer to achieve the right atmosphere—one that invites introspection and calm.

Creating a sacred space for reflection is an act of self-care, a physical manifestation of your commitment to personal growth and introspection. By carving out a dedicated spot for contemplation, you enrich your environment and affirm the importance of quiet, reflective time in your life. This space becomes a sanctuary where you can reconnect with yourself, gain clarity, and emerge rejuvenated and inspired.

Reflection as a Tool for Emotional Regulation

Reflection, looking inward and examining our thoughts and feelings, is a powerful tool for managing emotions. It allows us to step back, understand our emotional responses, and make more mindful decisions about handling them. Instead of being swept away by our feelings, reflective practices can help us navigate our dynamic landscape with grace and wisdom.

At the heart of using reflection for emotional regulation is the practice of mindfulness. By becoming more aware of our present thoughts and feelings without judgment, we can observe our emotions without becoming overwhelmed. This mindful observation creates a space between the surface and reacting to emotion, allowing us to choose how we respond.

Journaling is another reflective practice that can be incredibly effective for emotional regulation. Writing down your feelings can help clarify emotions that might feel tangled and confusing in your mind. You could become aware of triggers or patterns in your emotional reactions while writing that you were unaware of. This awareness can be enlightening, offering insights into how to manage similar situations better.

Another aspect of reflective emotional regulation involves questioning the stories we tell ourselves. Often, our emotions are fueled by narratives we've constructed about what's happening to us. By reflecting on these stories and asking ourselves whether they're entirely true, we can sometimes find that our emotional reactions are based on assumptions or misinterpretations. This realization can diffuse the intensity of our emotions, allowing us to approach situations more calmly and rationally.

Self-compassion is a crucial component of using reflection for emotional regulation. It's about showing oneself the same consideration and consideration that you would show a close friend. When reflecting on your emotions, especially those difficult or painful, approach them compassionately. Acknowledge that it's okay to feel what you're feeling and remind yourself that you're not alone in experiencing such emotions. This gentle approach can soothe distress and foster emotional healing.

Lastly, reflective practices can be enriched through dialogue with oneself or others. You may add depth and perspective to your knowledge by thinking things over silently, talking them out loud to yourself, or consulting a therapist or trusted friend. This verbal processing can help untangle complex feelings and lead to resolutions that are not apparent through silent reflection alone.

To sum up, contemplation is a strong friend on the path to emotional control. By adopting reflective practices such as mindfulness, journaling, questioning our narratives, practicing self-compassion, and engaging in dialogue, we can navigate our dynamic world more clearly, understanding, and effectively. These practices help manage our emotions in the moment and contribute to long-term emotional resilience and well-being.

CHAPTER 4

NURTURING SELF-CARE AND WELL-BEING

"Self-care is not a selfish act; it is a way to take care of our own needs so we can be healthy, happy, and able to support others."

- Audre Lorde

In the hustle and complexity of modern life, nurturing self-care and well-being has become an essential foundation for a balanced and fulfilling existence. This chapter delves into the art and importance of self-care, a practice that Audre Lorde so eloquently reminds us is not just an act of personal indulgence but a critical component of overall health and happiness. Here, we explore how self-care can be woven into our daily lives, offering strategies and insights to cultivate holistic well-being. From physical health to mental and emotional nourishment, this chapter guides embracing self-care practices that rejuvenate the body, mind, and soul, enabling us to lead more vibrant, purposeful lives.

The Spectrum of Self-care

Self-care has become ubiquitous in conversations about health and wellness, often conjuring up images of bubble baths, spa days, and indulgent moments of relaxation. While these activities can form part of a self-care routine, the spectrum of self-care is far broader, encompassing many practices that nurture the mind, body, and soul. By broadening our understanding of self-care, we can embrace a more holistic approach that caters to our diverse needs and leads to profound, lasting well-being.

Self-care is about taking proactive steps to care for your physical, mental, and emotional health. It involves committing to being aware of and attending to your needs, realizing that they are not extras but requirements for leading a healthy and satisfying life. This broadened concept of self-care involves several dimensions, each crucial to our overall well-being.

Physical Self-Care

Physical self-care is attending to your body and understanding its requirements. This includes exercise, nutrition, adequate sleep, personal hygiene, and healthcare. Regular physical activity, whether structured workouts, leisurely walks, or any form of movement you enjoy, is vital for maintaining physical health. Equally important is nourishing your body with foods that make you feel good and provide the necessary nutrients. Listening to your body's signals, whether hunger, fatigue, or pain, and responding appropriately is a fundamental aspect of physical self-care.

Mental Self-Care

Mental self-care is about maintaining a healthy and positive state of mind. This can involve practices like mindfulness and meditation to reduce stress and enhance focus, but it also includes engaging in activities that stimulate your intellect and curiosity. Reading, learning new skills, or even solving puzzles can all be forms of mental self-care. Additionally, setting boundaries to protect your mental space, such as limiting time on social media or saying no to commitments that overextend you, is crucial for mental wellness.

Emotional Self-Care

Emotional self-care focuses on acknowledging and processing your feelings healthily. It's about allowing yourself to feel whatever emotions arise without judgment and finding constructive ways to express and manage these feelings. This might involve journaling, talking with a trusted friend or therapist, or engaging in creative outlets like art or music. Cultivating a practice of self-compassion and forgiveness is also a significant aspect of emotional self-care, as it allows you to treat yourself with the same kindness you would offer others.

Social Self-Care

Humans are inherently social beings, and nurturing our relationships is vital to self-care. Social self-care involves investing time and energy in relationships that uplift and support you. It means prioritizing quality time with friends and family, seeking meaningful connections, and recognizing when certain relationships may harm your well-being and addressing them accordingly.

Spiritual Self-Care

For many, spiritual self-care is essential to feeling whole and connected. This can mean different things to different people: for some, it involves participation in organized religion, while for others, it might mean spending time in nature, meditating, or engaging in practices that foster a sense of connection to something greater than oneself. Whatever form it takes, spiritual self-care is about finding meaning and purpose in your life.

Professional Self-Care

Often overlooked, professional self-care is about managing work-related stress and finding fulfillment in your career. This includes setting clear boundaries around work hours, taking regular breaks, and seeking opportunities for growth and development. It's also about cultivating a positive work environment, whether decorating your workspace in a way that brings you joy or building supportive relationships with colleagues.

Embracing the broad spectrum of self-care requires a mindful approach to daily living that acknowledges the multifaceted nature of well-being. Integrating practices from each of these dimensions into our lives can build a comprehensive self-care routine that holistically supports our health and happiness. Remember, self-care is a deeply personal practice, and what works for one person may not work for another. The key is to explore various techniques, listen to your needs, and create a self-care plan that feels authentic and fulfilling.

Setting Realistic Self-care Goals

Talking about self-care often sounds like a beautiful, romantic plan we hope to incorporate into our daily lives. However, setting realistic self-care goals is essential for making these practices a part of our routine rather than just a wish list we never fulfill. Let's dive into how you can set achievable self-care goals, focusing on creating a balanced approach that genuinely enhances your well-being.

The first step in setting realistic self-care goals is understanding what self-care truly means for you. Developing a lifestyle that supports your mental, emotional, and physical health is more essential than just indulging yourself sometimes or escaping from everyday life. To do this, reflecting on your current life situation, needs, and challenges is crucial. Think about what aspects of your life could use more attention and care. Maybe you've been neglecting your need for quiet time, or perhaps your body is craving more movement.

Once you've identified your needs, the next step is to start small. This can't be emphasized enough. Often, we set grandiose goals for ourselves and become overwhelmed at the thought of trying to achieve them, leading to procrastination or abandoning the plan altogether. For example, if you've realized you need more physical activity, don't immediately commit to running five miles every morning. Instead, start with something more manageable, like a ten-minute walk daily or a short yoga session a few times a week. The key is to make it so doable that you can't find an excuse not to do it.

Incorporating self-care into your daily routine is another crucial aspect of setting achievable goals. Look at your typical day and identify pockets of time that could be used for self-care activities. Maybe it's a few minutes of deep breathing and mindfulness when you wake up, or it's dedicating the half-hour before bed to reading something uplifting instead of scrolling through social media. By embedding self-care into your schedule, it becomes part of the natural flow of your day rather than an added task you have to find time for.

Another important consideration is to be flexible with your self-care goals. Life is unpredictable, and there will be days when even the most well-planned routines go awry. On such days, be kind to yourself and adjust your expectations. If you miss your morning meditation, sit quietly for a few minutes during your lunch break. The goal is to maintain the intention behind your self-care practice, even if the execution isn't perfect.

Setting and meeting an accountability standard might be crucial to reaching your self-care objectives. Sharing your intentions with a friend or family member who can check in or join you in your self-care activities can provide an extra layer of motivation. Sometimes, knowing someone else knows your goals can push you to follow through.

Celebrating your successes, no matter how small, is vital. Did you manage to meditate for five minutes every day this week? That's fantastic! Reward yourself with something reinforcing the positive behavior, like a new book or a nice cup of coffee. Acknowledging your achievements helps to build momentum and enhances the value of your self-care practices.

Lastly, remember that setting realistic self-care goals is an ongoing process. As you grow and your life changes, your self-care needs will evolve. Regularly reevaluate your goals to ensure they still serve you well. That ten-minute walk is now too easy, and you're ready to increase it to twenty minutes. Or you've found that journaling in the evening brings you more peace than you anticipated, and you want to make it a more significant part of your routine.

Setting realistic self-care goals is about making small, manageable changes that can be easily integrated into your daily life. It's about being kind and flexible with yourself and recognizing that the path to well-being is a marathon, not a sprint. You may develop a sustainable self-care routine that promotes your general well-being by taking the time to identify your requirements, starting small, adding self-care to your daily activities, and appreciating your accomplishments.

The Importance of Community in Self-care

Self-care often conjures images of solo activities—meditation in a quiet room, a solitary walk in nature, or a peaceful evening with a book. However, an essential aspect of self-care that sometimes goes unnoticed is the role of community. Human beings are inherently social creatures, and our connections with others are crucial to our overall well-being. Finding communities for shared self-care can significantly enhance the effectiveness of our self-care practices, offering support, motivation, and a sense of belonging.

The importance of community in self-care cannot be overstated. We are part of a community, whether a yoga class, a book club, or a gardening group, that connects us to others who share our interests and values. These connections provide a network of support that can be incredibly comforting, especially during challenging times. Sharing experiences, challenges, and successes with others reminds us that we're not alone in our struggles, making our burdens feel lighter.

Communities offer unique perspectives and insights that can enrich our self-care journey. Engaging in discussions, sharing tips, and listening to others' experiences can introduce us to new self-care practices we haven't yet considered. This exchange of ideas broadens our self-care repertoire and encourages us to think critically about what practices best suit our needs.

Participating in group activities can also boost our motivation to maintain self-care routines. When you know others are counting on your participation, it's often easier to commit to a meditation session, a workout, or a healthy cooking class. The accountability that comes with community involvement can be a powerful motivator, helping us stick to our self-care goals even when our motivation wanes.

Moreover, communities provide social self-care opportunities—nurturing our need for human connection. Engaging in activities with others fulfills our social needs, contributing to our emotional and mental health. Because they provide a sense of acceptance and belonging, these connections can benefit people who suffer from loneliness or isolation.

However, finding the right community for shared self-care can be challenging. It takes work and a readiness to move outside our comfort zones. Here are a few strategies to help you find communities that align with your self-care needs:

1. Identify Your Interests: Consider what activities you enjoy or are curious about. Whether it's fitness, mindfulness, art, or environmental conservation, knowing what you're passionate about will guide your search for relevant communities.

2. Explore Local and Online Options: Look for community centers, gyms, libraries, or online platforms that offer groups or classes related to your interests. Many communities have moved online, providing forums, virtual meetups, and lessons accessible from anywhere.

3. Attend Events and Meetups: Once you've identified potential communities, take the plunge and attend a few events or meetings. It might initially feel intimidating, but remember that everyone in these spaces is there for similar reasons—to connect and engage in shared activities.

4. Be Open and Patient: Finding the right community can take time. Be open to trying different groups and activities until you find one that feels like a good fit. Remember, the goal is to enhance your self-care practice, so look for communities where you feel welcomed and supported.

5. Create Your Own: If you need help finding a community that meets your needs, consider starting your own. Whether it's a walking group in your neighborhood or an online book club, creating a space for shared interests can be a rewarding way to build your community.

Incorporating community into your self-care practice can transform how you approach well-being, offering support, inspiration, and connection. While self-care often involves personal reflection and solo activities, the strength, motivation, and joy we derive from being part of a community remind us that we're part of something larger than ourselves. Nurturing these connections enhances our self-care practices but also contributes to the well-being of others, creating a cycle of support and care that benefits us all.

Holistic Approaches to Self-care

Self-care is more than just treating ourselves to occasional indulgences; it's about taking comprehensive care of every part of our being—body, mind, and spirit. A holistic approach to self-care involves integrating practices that nourish us physically, mentally, and spiritually, creating a balance that supports overall well-being. Let's explore how we can weave these elements into a cohesive self-care routine, ensuring we care for all aspects of ourselves.

Physical Self-Care: Nurturing the Body

Physical self-care is the most visible form of self-care. It entails consistent exercise, a balanced diet, enough sleep, and regular medical treatment that supports and enhances physical health. Exercise doesn't have to mean hours at the gym; it can be anything that gets your body moving and you enjoy—dancing, walking, yoga, or even gardening. Eating nutritious foods nourishes your body and gives you the energy you need to tackle your day, while adequate sleep restores and heals your body and mind. Regular check-ups and being proactive about health concerns are also crucial to physical self-care.

Mental Self-Care: Nurturing the Mind

Mental self-care focuses on maintaining a healthy and positive mental state. This includes managing stress, engaging in activities that challenge and stimulate the mind, and practicing mindfulness and meditation to achieve mental clarity and peace. Finding stress-relief techniques that work for you through deep breathing exercises, journaling, or creative outlets like painting or writing is essential. Stimulating the mind by learning new things, reading, or solving puzzles can also improve mental well-being. Being aware may help you stay in the present and enjoy it, which lowers anxiety and improves your mood in general.

Spiritual Self-Care: Nurturing the Spirit

Spiritual self-care is connecting with your inner self and finding more profound meaning and purpose. This doesn't necessarily mean religion, though for some, religious practices are a significant aspect of their spiritual self-care. It can also involve time in nature, meditation, practicing gratitude, or engaging in activities connecting you to something greater than yourself. Spiritual self-care is profoundly personal and can look different for everyone; it's about finding what feeds your soul and brings you inner peace.

Integrating These Practices

The key to holistic self-care is integration—finding ways to incorporate physical, mental, and spiritual self-care into your daily routine in a seamless and manageable way. One way to do this is to look for activities that cover multiple areas of self-care at once. For example, yoga can be a physical exercise that offers mental relaxation and spiritual connection. Similarly, spending time in nature can be physically stimulating, mentally refreshing, and spiritually fulfilling.

It's also important to listen to your body and mind and recognize that your self-care needs might change daily. Some days, your body may need more rest, while your mind might crave stimulation from others. Flexibility and responsiveness to your needs are crucial in a holistic self-care practice.

Another aspect of integrating holistic self-care into your life is setting realistic goals and prioritizing self-care. This might mean scheduling self-care activities into your day or setting boundaries with work and relationships to ensure you have time for self-care. Remember, self-care is not selfish; caring for yourself allows you to show up more fully in your relationships and responsibilities.

Lastly, remember that holistic self-care is a journey, not a destination. It involves ongoing learning and adjustment as you discover what practices best support your well-being. It's about treating yourself with kindness and compassion and recognizing that caring for your body, mind, and spirit is essential for a balanced and fulfilling life.

Making self-care a comprehensive endeavor can help you ensure you're thriving rather than just surviving. Integrating physical, mental, and spiritual practices into your routine can help you achieve balance and well-being that radiates into all areas of your life, allowing you to live more fully and joyfully.

Prioritizing Self-care in Busy Schedules

Maintaining a self-care routine amidst a bustling schedule can seem like an uphill battle in today's fast-paced world. However, prioritizing self-care, even during the busiest times, is crucial for sustaining our health, well-being, and productivity. Here are some strategies for keeping self-care at the forefront of your life, no matter how packed your calendar might be.

Firstly, shifting our perspective on self-care from a luxury to a necessity is essential. The first step is recognizing that taking care of yourself is not selfish but essential for functioning at your best. This mindset change can make it easier to justify carving out time for self-care activities, even during busy periods.

One practical approach is to integrate self-care into your daily routines. This means finding ways to include self-care activities in the tasks you're already doing. For instance, practice mindfulness while showering or drinking coffee if you have a hectic morning. It's about making self-care a seamless part of your day rather than requiring additional time and effort.

Like any other important appointment, planning and scheduling self-care activities can also make a significant difference. Look at your week ahead and identify slots where you can realistically fit in some form of self-care, whether it's a 15-minute walk, a quick meditation session, or time to read before bed. By scheduling these activities, you commit yourself to maintaining these practices, making it more likely that you'll stick to them.

Learning to say no is another vital strategy for prioritizing self-care during busy times. Often, our schedules become overloaded because we take on more than we can manage. By setting boundaries and being selective about the commitments you agree to, you can free up more time for activities that nourish and recharge you. Remember, whenever you say yes to something, you're saying no to something else, potentially your self-care.

Seeking out brief daily opportunities to care for yourself is another beneficial strategy. You don't only sometimes need large blocks of time to care for yourself. Even short periods can be incredibly helpful. This might involve doing breathing exercises during a five-minute break at work, enjoying a healthy snack, or stretching between tasks. These small acts of self-care can accumulate, significantly impacting your well-being over time.

Embracing flexibility in your self-care routine is crucial, especially during busy times. Your ability to maintain certain self-care practices might vary from day to day, and that's okay. Be kind to yourself and adjust your self-care practices as needed. What's important is maintaining the intention behind your self-care, even if the specific activities change.

Finally, enlisting support from friends, family, or colleagues can help you maintain your self-care routine. Share your goals with them and ask for their support, whether joining you for a walk, respecting your need for quiet time in the evening, or simply offering encouragement. Knowing that others know and support your self-care efforts can provide additional motivation to prioritize these practices.

Maintaining a self-care routine during busy times requires intention, planning, and creativity. By integrating self-care into your daily routines, scheduling self-care activities, setting boundaries, finding small moments for self-care, embracing flexibility, and seeking support, you can ensure that taking care of yourself remains a top priority. Remember, self-care is the foundation for building your productivity, happiness, and well-being. Prioritizing it, even during the busiest times, is essential for living a balanced and fulfilling life.

CHAPTER 5

"Resilience is not about how you endure. It's about how you recharge."

- Sheryl Sandberg

In the journey of life, challenges and obstacles are inevitable. It's not the presence of these hurdles that defines us but how we respond and grow from them. Chapter 5 delves into the heart of resilience, the extraordinary capacity to bounce back from adversity more muscular and determined. Drawing inspiration from Sheryl Sandberg's insightful perspective on resilience, this chapter explores the essence of enduring life's trials and emerging from them with renewed strength and wisdom. Here, we'll learn resilience-building techniques and approaches that help us deal with life's ups and downs gracefully and adaptably. Through understanding and cultivating resilience, we arm ourselves with the tools to face challenges head-on and recharge our spirits, ready to embrace whatever comes next with open arms and a resilient heart.

Developing a Resilient Mindset: Strategies for Mental Resilience

Developing a resilient mindset is like building a muscle; it requires practice, patience, and persistence. A resilient mindset allows us to face life's challenges with strength and grace, bouncing back from setbacks more robust than before. Here's how to cultivate mental resilience and prepare to navigate challenging times more effectively.

Understand That Setbacks Are Part of Life

To cultivate a resilient attitude, one must first acknowledge that obstacles, setbacks, and failures are inevitable aspects of life. Nobody sails through life without facing some form of adversity. This removes the unrealistic expectation that life should be smooth and free of obstacles, making you better prepared to face challenges head-on.

Focus on What You Can Control

In any challenging situation, there are aspects we can control and those we cannot. Resilient people focus their energy on what they can control—their responses to the problem. Concentrating on your actions and reactions empowers you to make positive changes rather than feeling helpless against the circumstances.

Maintain a Positive Outlook

Maintaining a positive outlook doesn't mean ignoring reality or pretending everything is fine when it isn't. It's about focusing on the positives and having faith in overcoming obstacles. This positive outlook is crucial for resilience, as it motivates you to look for solutions rather than dwelling on problems.

Build Strong Relationships

Resilience is not just an individual trait; it's also nurtured by the support and love of those around us. Building solid and supportive relationships ensures you have a network to lean on during tough times. Feel free to reach out for help or offer support to others. Mutual support strengthens resilience, reminding us we're not alone in our struggles.

Take Care of Your Physical Health

Our physical well-being dramatically influences our mental toughness—healthy eating, regular exercise, and enough sleep support a more assertive, robust attitude. Physical activity, in particular, reduces stress and improves mood, making it easier to cope with challenges.

Practice Mindfulness and Stress Reduction Techniques

Deep breathing exercises, yoga, and other mindfulness and stress-reduction practices can all significantly increase resilience. These practices help calm the mind, reduce stress, and improve emotional regulation, enabling you to approach challenges with a more evident, focused mindset.

Set Realistic Goals and Take Action

Resilience depends on having a feeling of purpose and direction, which may be fostered by setting reasonable objectives and working toward them. Break down more considerable challenges into manageable tasks and celebrate small victories. Action breeds confidence and diminishes feelings of helplessness, bolstering your resilience.

Learn from Your Experiences

Resilient people see obstacles as chances to improve. Reflect on past experiences and consider what they've taught you. By learning from your setbacks, you become better equipped to handle future challenges and develop a deeper appreciation for your strengths and capabilities.

Cultivate Gratitude

Being grateful may change your attention from what's wrong in your life to what is going well. Make it a habit to acknowledge and appreciate the good, even in difficult times. This practice can change your perspective, making maintaining hope and resilience in adversity easier.

Embrace Change

Change is often uncomfortable, but it's also inevitable. Embracing change rather than resisting it can reduce the stress and anxiety of new situations. Resilient people adapt to change, using it as an opportunity to learn and grow.

Developing a resilient mindset is a journey that involves embracing challenges, learning from them, and continuously striving to improve oneself. By implementing these strategies, you'll build your ability to overcome setbacks and create the foundation for a better, happier life. Remember, resilience doesn't mean never falling; it means always being willing to get back up and try again.

Learning from Failure: Viewing failures as growth opportunities

Failure is an experience we all face, yet it holds different meanings for everyone. Some see it as an endpoint, a signal to give up, while others consider it a crucial step to success. The latter perspective, seeing failure as a growth opportunity, is a powerful mindset that can transform our approach to challenges and setbacks.

When we encounter failure, it's natural to feel disappointed, discouraged, or even heartbroken. These feelings are valid, but they don't have to define our next steps. Instead, we can see failure as a lesson, a chance to learn something about ourselves, our methods, or our goals. This shift in perspective isn't easy, but it's gratifying.

Think of a toddler learning to walk. They don't stand up and stride across the room on their first try. They fall, sometimes softly, sometimes with a bump. But with each fall, they learn. They adjust their balance, strength, and technique. They keep trying until one day; walking is second nature. This process of learning and adapting is similar to how we can approach failure at any age.

One key to learning from failure is reflection. After a setback:

- Take some time to think about what happened.
- Ask yourself what went wrong, but also look for what you did right.

Consider what factors were within your control and which weren't. This reflection can help you identify changes you might make next time, whether adjusting your approach, seeking additional resources, or even reevaluating your goals.

Another vital aspect is openness to feedback. Sometimes, our perspective on our failures is limited. Feedback from others can offer new insights and ideas on how to move forward. It's crucial, however, to seek input from those who are supportive and constructive rather than critical and discouraging.

It's also beneficial to reframe how we talk to ourselves about failure. Instead of harsh self-criticism, try speaking to yourself with compassion and encouragement, as you would talk to a friend in a similar situation. This self-compassion can be a source of strength, helping you to persist despite setbacks.

Sharing your experiences with failure can also be enlightening. Often, we hide our failures, fearing judgment or embarrassment. However, sharing them can provide relief and connect us with others who have faced similar challenges. These shared experiences can offer comfort, advice, and, sometimes, a good laugh over the absurdities that sometimes accompany our efforts.

Moreover, embracing a mindset of curiosity can transform failure from a dreaded outcome to an exciting puzzle. View each failure as a question: "What can I learn from this?" This curiosity can drive innovation and creativity, leading to solutions and approaches you might never have considered otherwise.

Finally, it's crucial to celebrate the effort, not just the outcome. Recognizing the hard work, courage, and determination it takes to pursue our goals can help build resilience. This recognition reinforces that while we may not control every outcome, we have control over our efforts and attitudes.

Learning from failure is about shifting our focus from what we've lost to what we can gain. It's about recognizing that each setback is a stepping stone, not a stumbling block. This perspective doesn't just apply to significant, life-altering failures but to the small, everyday ones as well. Every mistake in a project, every missed opportunity in a relationship, and every goal not yet achieved can teach us something valuable.

Adopting this mindset requires patience and practice. But the more we learn to see failure as a growth opportunity, the more resilient, innovative, and persistent we become. We start to fear failure less, knowing that each misstep brings us closer to our goals. Perhaps most importantly, we learn that our worth is not defined by our failures or successes but by the courage to keep trying, learning, and growing, no matter the outcome.

Building a Support System for Resilience

Building a support system is like constructing a safety net for when life throws us into freefall. It's about surrounding ourselves with people who provide emotional, mental, and sometimes even physical support. This network isn't just a buffer against life's challenges; it's a foundation that enables us to bounce back more quickly and with greater strength. Let's delve into how creating a solid support network can enhance resilience and the steps we can take to cultivate such relationships.

First and foremost, recognizing the value of diverse support is critical. A robust support system includes various people—family members, friends, colleagues, mentors, and even professionals like therapists or counselors. Each offers different perspectives, resources, and types of support. Family and friends provide love and emotional comfort, colleagues and mentors offer advice and professional guidance, and therapists give expert, unbiased support for mental health challenges.

Opening up to others about our needs and struggles is often the first, and sometimes the most challenging, step in building a support system. It requires vulnerability, which many of us find daunting. However, sharing our experiences helps us feel less alone and invites others to share their own stories, deepening mutual understanding and connection. It's critical to remember that asking for help is a calculated step toward resilience rather than a show of weakness.

Cultivating these relationships takes time and effort. Consistent communication, showing appreciation for the support received, and being there for others in their time of need all contribute to more robust, reliable connections. Activities that foster bonding, such as shared hobbies, regular check-ins, and celebrating each other's successes, also strengthen these ties.

Another vital aspect of building a support system is setting boundaries. Mutual respect and an awareness of one another's limitations are the cornerstones of healthy partnerships. Communicating your needs clearly and respecting others' boundaries ensures that the support system remains positive and beneficial.

Expanding your support network might be necessary, especially if you're facing challenges your current circle needs help understanding or assisting with. Joining support groups, clubs, or online communities related to your experiences or interests can introduce you to people with similar situations or goals. These new connections can offer fresh insights, empathy, and strategies for coping that you might not have considered.

Learning to support others is just as important as seeking support for yourself. Providing encouragement, listening actively, and offering help when needed benefit those you care for and reinforce your sense of purpose and connection. Moreover, it fosters a reciprocal environment where everyone feels valued and supported.

Lastly, it's crucial to periodically evaluate your support system as your needs and circumstances change over time. Some relationships may naturally drift apart, while others become more central to your life. This evaluation helps ensure that your network remains aligned with your current needs and values, providing the most effective support for your resilience.

Building a support system for resilience is more than just having people to lean on during tough times. It's about creating a mutual support, respect, and growth community. By actively cultivating these relationships, we enhance our ability to weather life's storms and contribute to a culture of compassion and resilience that uplifts everyone involved. This support network becomes a source of strength for facing challenges, pursuing opportunities, and celebrating life's joys together.

Cultivating Patience and Perseverance

Cultivating patience and perseverance is like planting seeds in a garden. As seeds require time, care, and the right conditions to grow, so do these qualities within us. They are necessary for resilience because they help us deal with the highs and lows of life with grace and tenacity. Developing patience and perseverance is a journey that enriches our character and strengthens our capacity to face challenges.

Patience, the ability to wait calmly in the face of frustration or adversity, is a cornerstone of resilience. It allows us to endure difficult situations without becoming agitated or losing hope. Cultivating patience starts with acknowledging that things often don't happen on our preferred timeline. Life is unpredictable, and delays and obstacles are part of the journey. By accepting this, we learn to approach situations calmly and open-mindedly, reducing stress and making more thoughtful decisions.

Deep breathing exercises and other mindfulness techniques are valuable methods for cultivating patience. These practices help us become more aware of our thoughts and feelings in the moment, allowing us to respond to situations with clarity rather than react impulsively. Over time, mindfulness teaches us to appreciate the present, even when challenging, fostering a more profound sense of patience.

Conversely, perseverance is the unwavering commitment to a task in the face of adversity or a delay in reaching achievement. It's about pushing through obstacles, not with blind stubbornness, but with a focused and persistent effort towards a goal. Developing perseverance begins with setting meaningful goals that align with our values and aspirations. When our goals resonate deeply with us, we're more motivated to overcome the challenges that arise on the path to achieving them.

Perseverance may also be cultivated by dividing complex objectives into minor, more doable activities. Celebrating small victories along the way keeps our spirits up and maintains momentum, even when progress seems slow. This approach makes daunting challenges feel more achievable, reinforcing our commitment to persist.

Having a development mentality is also essential for developing perseverance. This entails seeing difficulties as opportunities to create and learn rather than insurmountable barriers. When we embrace the possibility of growth, setbacks become less discouraging and more like stepping stones on the path to success. This mindset encourages us to keep trying, experimenting, and learning, which is essential to perseverance.

Support from others can also significantly contribute to developing patience and perseverance. Sharing our struggles and successes with friends, family, or mentors can provide encouragement, advice, and a different perspective. Knowing we're not alone in our journey can make staying patient and persevering through tough times more manageable.

Moreover, self-compassion is crucial in cultivating these qualities. Being kind to ourselves when things are unplanned helps us maintain patience and perseverance. It allows us to acknowledge our efforts, learn from our mistakes, and move forward without harsh self-judgment.

Finally, cultivating patience and perseverance requires regular reflection. Reflecting on our experiences and challenges and how we've grown from them can provide valuable insights. It helps us recognize our progress, understand our resilience, and appreciate the role of patience and perseverance in our achievements.

Developing patience and perseverance is a transformative process that enhances our resilience. These qualities enable us to face life's challenges with confidence and grace, secure in the knowledge that we can endure setbacks and persist toward our goals. Like the seeds in a garden, patience and perseverance need time and care to flourish, but the strength and resilience they foster are well worth the effort. By embracing mindfulness, setting meaningful goals, adopting a growth mindset, seeking support, practicing self-compassion, and reflecting on our journey, we can cultivate these essential qualities and navigate the path of life with resilience and determination.

Resilience through Self-Compassion

Resilience and self-compassion are two sides of the same coin, though they may seem like distant concepts at first glance. While self-compassion is the ability to treat oneself with care and understanding while facing failure or sadness, resilience is the ability to withstand hardship. When woven together, self-compassion becomes a powerful catalyst for resilience, offering a gentle yet profound way to navigate life's challenges.

Self-compassion involves three key components: mindfulness, common humanity, and self-kindness. Mindfulness allows us to recognize our pain or suffering without over-identifying it. It helps us to acknowledge our feelings and experiences without letting them define us. Common humanity connects our experiences of failure or difficulty with those of others, reminding us that we are not alone in our struggles. Lastly, self-kindness encourages us to be gentle and understanding with ourselves rather than harshly self-critical.

Integrating self-compassion into our lives begins with changing the way we talk to ourselves. Often, we are our own harshest critics, especially when we face setbacks. By consciously shifting our internal dialogue to one of kindness and support, we can alleviate much of the additional suffering we create for ourselves. Instead of criticizing ourselves for mistakes or failures, we can offer encouragement, just as we would to a close friend in a similar situation.

Self-compassion also teaches us that failure and suffering are part of the human experience. This understanding can dramatically change our perspective on setbacks. Rather than viewing difficulties as personal failures, we can see them as universal experiences that connect us to others. This shift fosters a sense of belonging and reduces feelings of isolation during tough times, making it easier to bounce back.

Moreover, self-compassion provides emotional resilience by allowing us to hold space for our pain and treat ourselves kindly. It encourages a balanced approach to handling our emotions, neither suppressing nor exaggerating our pain. This balance is crucial for moving through challenges without getting stuck in negative spirals that can hinder our recovery and growth.

Practicing self-compassion can also lead to more extraordinary perseverance and courage. When we know we will treat ourselves with kindness and understanding, regardless of the outcome, we're more likely to take risks and step out of our comfort zones. This willingness to be vulnerable and try new things, even when there's a chance of failure, is a hallmark of resilience.

Various techniques may be used to develop self-compassion, including guided meditations, writing letters to oneself with compassion, or taking little breaks during the day to check in with oneself and provide love. Regular practice helps to reinforce the habit of self-compassion, making it a natural response to adversity.

Self-compassion is not a luxury but a necessity in the journey of building resilience. It is the gentle hand that helps us up when we fall, the soothing voice that encourages us to try again, and the warm embrace that reminds us we're not alone. We discover via self-compassion that our value is based on our commitment to treat ourselves with love and respect regardless of the challenges life presents, not on our accomplishments or shortcomings. By nurturing self-compassion, we don't just survive challenges; we grow from them, emerging stronger, wiser, and more connected to ourselves and the world around us.

CHAPTER 6

UNLEASHING CREATIVITY AND EXPRESSING YOUR AUTHENTIC VOICE

"Creativity is the way I share my soul with the world."

- Brené Brown

In the tapestry of human experience, creativity emerges as a vibrant thread, weaving together expressions of our deepest thoughts, feelings, and insights. Chapter 6, "Unleashing Creativity and Expressing Your Authentic Voice," invites us to explore the boundless landscapes of our imagination and the unique expressions of our inner selves. Drawing inspiration from Brené Brown's eloquent reflection on creativity, this chapter delves into the transformative power of creative expression in revealing and celebrating our authentic selves. Through the following pages, we'll discover strategies and practices to unlock our creative potential, overcome barriers to creativity, and find joy in the authentic expression of our thoughts and feelings. Creativity is an artistic endeavor and a way of living authentically, a path to understanding ourselves and sharing our unique perspective with the world.

Creative Routines and Rituals

Creating a life enriched with creativity isn't just about having sporadic moments of inspiration; it's about nurturing a daily environment that invites and cultivates creative thinking. Establishing creative routines and rituals can be transformative, turning the elusive muse of inspiration into a constant, reliable companion.

Think of creativity not as a rare, fleeting visitor but as a seed within you that requires consistent care and attention to flourish. You may establish routines that support your creative spirit, such as a gardener tending to their garden with daily rituals to ensure its flourishing. The beauty of these routines and habits is that they can be tailored to fit your unique lifestyle, preferences, and innovative aspirations.

One of the first steps in cultivating a creative routine is to set aside dedicated time for creativity. This doesn't mean you must carve out hours from your busy day; even just a few minutes can make a difference. The key is consistency. Whether waking up 15 minutes earlier to jot down ideas in a journal, sketching during your lunch break, or dedicating time before bed to play an instrument, these moments can significantly impact your creative output.

Creating a physical space dedicated to your creative endeavors can also spark inspiration. This doesn't require an elaborate studio; a small corner of your room, a desk with your materials, or even a portable box containing your tools can serve as your creative sanctuary. Entering this space signals to your brain that it's time to focus on creative work, helping to shift your mindset and prepare you for productive sessions.

Incorporating rituals into your creative practice can also significantly enhance creativity. Traditions include brewing tea, lighting a candle, or playing a specific song before beginning a creative activity. These actions help transition from the ordinary tasks of daily life into a creative mindset, signaling to your subconscious that it's time to focus on creative endeavors.

Another successful tactic is participating in activities that appear unconnected to your creative pursuits but are proven to foster creative thinking. Walking, engaging in mindfulness exercises, or even doing menial chores like cleaning the dishes can give your subconscious the mental space to work on creative challenges, resulting in breakthroughs and unexpected discoveries.

It is also beneficial to feed your creativity with a steady diet of inspiration. This means exposing yourself to various ideas, experiences, and artistic expressions. Reading books, visiting galleries, attending performances, or exploring nature can fuel creativity. Keeping an idea journal to jot down thoughts, observations, and inspirations can help you capture fleeting ideas to explore later in your dedicated creative time.

Lastly, be open to experimentation within your routines and rituals. The creative process is inherently about exploration and discovery, and what works for one person may not work for another. Feel free to try new routines, adjust your rituals, and explore different creative mediums. This openness can lead to unexpected sources of inspiration and innovation in your work.

In essence, establishing creative routines and rituals is about committing to your creative practice and regularly honoring that commitment. It's about recognizing the value of creativity in your life and taking intentional steps to nurture it. Doing so creates a fertile ground for your imagination to grow, ensuring that your authentic voice finds its expression in the world. This approach transforms creativity from a sporadic occurrence into a vibrant, integral part of your daily life, enriching your experiences and offering new perspectives on the world around you.

Overcoming Creative Blocks

Every creative individual faces a challenge at some point: Navigating creative slumps. These periods, characterized by a lack of inspiration or motivation, can feel like hitting an invisible wall, preventing you from expressing your ideas and visions. However, overcoming creative blocks is possible and can be a valuable part of your creative journey, offering opportunities for growth and discovery. Here are some tips for overcoming these slumps and reigniting your creative spark.

Step Away and Take a Break

Sometimes, the best thing to do when facing a creative block is to step away from your work. Continuous effort without breaks can lead to burnout, making creative blocks even more challenging. Taking a break, whether a short walk outside, a day off, or a vacation, can provide new perspectives and rejuvenate your creative energy.

Change Your Environment

Getting a fresh perspective significantly boosts your creative flow. If you work in the same area daily, think about switching to a new room, going outside, or going to a café or library. You can generate fresh thoughts and perceptions in a new area.

Seek New Experiences

Engaging in new experiences broadens your horizons and feeds your creativity. Try something outside your comfort zone, whether it's a new hobby, traveling to an unfamiliar place, or simply exploring a new genre of books or music. These encounters can offer novel concepts and viewpoints that might assist in overcoming a creativity barrier.

Connect with Others

Talking to other creative individuals can provide encouragement, inspiration, and valuable feedback. Sharing your struggles and successes with peers can remind you that creative blocks are a normal part of the creative process. Collaborating on projects or brainstorming sessions can generate new ideas and solutions you might not have considered.

Limit Distractions

In today's digital age, distractions are everywhere, constantly vying for our attention. These distractions can exacerbate creative blocks by preventing deep, focused work. Consider reducing your time on social media, disabling notifications, or designating particular times to check your emails and texts. A distraction-free environment can help you concentrate and reconnect with your creative flow.

Experiment with Different Creative Outlets

Sometimes, switching to a different creative medium can help overcome a block. If you're a writer struggling with writer's block, try drawing, painting, or playing an instrument. Engaging in a different creative activity can stimulate your brain in new ways, potentially unlocking the creativity you've been trying to access in your primary medium.

Practice Mindfulness and Meditation

Mindfulness and meditation, which can also help lower tension and increase attention, may simplify the process of overcoming mental obstacles to creativity. Regular practice of focused breathing or meditation, even briefly, can help cultivate clarity and serenity that will foster creativity.

Revisit Past Work

Looking back at your previous creative projects can remind you of your capabilities and achievements. It can also provide insights into your creative process, helping you identify patterns or techniques that have worked well for you in the past. Sometimes, the inspiration you need can be found in your portfolio.

Set Small, Achievable Goals

When faced with a creative block, the thought of completing a large project can feel overwhelming. Break your project into small, manageable tasks, and focus on completing one at a time. Achieving these smaller goals can build momentum and gradually lead you out of your creative slump.

Be Kind to Yourself

Lastly, it's important to practice self-compassion during creative blocks. Avoid harsh self-criticism and remind yourself that these periods are temporary and part of the creative process. Treating yourself with kindness and understanding can ease the pressure and help you find your way back to creativity.

Creative blocks, while frustrating, are manageable. By adopting these strategies, you can navigate these slumps with resilience and openness, often emerging on the other side with renewed creativity and a deeper understanding of your creative self. Remember, every creative journey has its highs and lows, and it's through overcoming these challenges that we grow as artists and individuals.

Sharing Your Creative Works

Sharing your creative works can be as daunting as it is exhilarating. Putting your creativity out into the world exposes you to feedback and criticism and, most importantly, connects you to others who might find inspiration or solace in your work. Confidently sharing your creative expressions is a significant step in your creative journey, one that acknowledges the value of your voice and vision. Here's how to embrace this process, navigate its vulnerabilities, and confidently share your creativity.

Understanding the value of your work is the foundation of sharing it confidently. Every piece you create reflects your unique perspective, experiences, and skills. Remember, creativity in itself is an act of courage. By creating, you're contributing to the vast tapestry of human expression, adding your distinct thread to the collective narrative. Recognizing this can bolster your confidence, reminding you that your work has inherent value simply because it is yours.

Preparation is vital before sharing your work. This means refining your piece to a state you feel proud of—not necessarily perfect, but reflective of your intentions and efforts. It also involves researching the best platforms or forums to share your work, whether a local art gallery, an online community, a blog, or social media. Choose platforms aligning with your goals and where your work will be appreciated and understood.

Building a supportive community around you can also enhance your confidence in sharing your work. Connect with fellow creators who understand the vulnerabilities of creative expression. This community can offer constructive feedback, encouragement, and advice based on their experiences. Moreover, being part of a creative community provides a sense of belonging, reinforcing that you're not alone in your creative endeavors.

Learning to detach your self-worth from the reception of your work is crucial. Only some pieces will be well-received, and that's okay. Creativity is subjective, and what resonates with one person might not with another. Please focus on the process of creating and the personal growth it brings rather than the outcome or reception. This mindset shift can significantly reduce the fear of sharing and encourage you to express yourself authentically.

Feedback is an inevitable part of sharing your work. Approach feedback with openness and a desire to learn, distinguishing between constructive criticism that can help you grow and negative feedback that doesn't serve your development. Remember, you don't have to agree with or act on all feedback, but considering different perspectives can be invaluable for your creative evolution.

Finally, celebrate the act of sharing itself, regardless of the outcome. Whenever you share your work, you take a brave step towards vulnerability and connection. Acknowledge the strength it takes to expose your creativity to the world and view each sharing experience as an achievement.

Confidently sharing your creative expressions is a journey that involves recognizing the value of your work, preparing thoroughly, building a supportive community, detaching your self-worth from external validation, navigating feedback constructively, and celebrating the courage it takes to share. By embracing these approaches, you can share your creativity more confidently, contributing your unique voice to the collective creative dialogue.

Exploring Multiple Creative Outlets: Encouraging experimentation with various forms of creativity

Diving into different creative activities is like exploring a treasure chest full of surprises. You only know what you'll discover about yourself once you try something new. Exploring multiple creative outlets is not just about making art or music; it's about letting your imagination run wild in various arenas, from writing and painting to gardening and cooking. This journey of experimentation can enrich your life, giving you fresh perspectives and enhancing your overall creative expression.

Sticking to just one creative path makes it easy to feel stuck or uninspired. That's where trying out different forms of creativity comes in. Each creative activity uses other parts of your brain, challenges you uniquely, and can spark ideas that transfer beautifully across various mediums. For example, the rhythm you feel while drumming might inspire a pattern in a painting, or the colors in a sunset you try to capture through photography could influence the mood of a story you're writing.

Starting this journey can be as simple as picking up something that piques your interest, but this is your first time trying. It requires a minimal investment in materials or classes. You can begin with free online tutorials, borrow supplies from a friend, or even start with digital forms of creation that only need software or apps. The key is approaching this exploration with a playful attitude, seeing it as a fun experiment rather than something you need to be perfect at.

One of the joys of exploring multiple creative outlets is the freedom from the pressure of being good. Since you're starting, there's no expectation to create a masterpiece. This freedom allows you to focus on the process of creation, which is where creativity's absolute joy and therapeutic benefits lie. You learn to appreciate your progress and celebrate small victories, like mastering a chord on the guitar or finishing a simple knitting project.

As you dive into different creative activities, you'll likely find that some resonate with you more than others. This discovery process is invaluable, helping you understand your preferences, strengths, and areas where you enjoy challenges. After giving them a fair shot, it's perfectly okay to decide that certain activities aren't for you. The goal isn't to become a jack-of-all-trades but to enrich your creative life by finding multiple outlets that bring you joy and satisfaction.

Exploring various forms of creativity also enhances your problem-solving skills and adaptability. Each creative domain comes with its own set of challenges and constraints. Learning to navigate these can make you a more versatile thinker, capable of applying innovative solutions in different areas of your life, not just in artistic projects.

Moreover, experimenting with multiple creative outlets can lead to unexpected connections and innovations. You might combine elements from different disciplines to create something unique, like incorporating poetry into visual art or using dance movements to inspire a sculpture. These cross-pollinations of ideas can lead to exciting new forms of expression that you might never have discovered if you hadn't ventured beyond your primary creative interest.

Talking about your exploratory trip with others may be a great way to get support and ideas. Whether through social media, a blog, or a local community group, connecting with like-minded individuals and experimenting with different creative activities can provide motivation, feedback, and a sense of camaraderie. You may find opportunities for collaboration that can further expand your creative horizons.

Exploring multiple creative outlets is a journey of curiosity, discovery, and growth. It's about permitting yourself to play, make mistakes, and learn in various creative fields. This exploration can deepen your appreciation for creativity in all its forms, enrich your creative pursuits, and open new avenues for expression and innovation. So, grab a pen, paintbrush, camera, or any tool that catches your fancy, and start experimenting. The world of creativity is vast and varied, and it's waiting for you to dive in and discover its treasures.

The Connection Between Creativity and Emotion

The intricate dance between creativity and emotion is as ancient as human expression. Our emotions, those profound and often inexplicable feelings that color our experiences, significantly influence our creative output. This connection isn't just about the emotional content of creative works but how emotions fuel the creative process, shaping ideas and inspiring innovation. Delving into this relationship offers insights into the power of emotions in unlocking our creative potential.

At the heart of creativity lies the ability to see the world differently, to imagine what might be instead of what is. Emotions play a crucial role in this process by affecting our perception, focus, and the associations we make. Positive emotions like joy and love often expand our perspective, making us more open to new experiences and ideas. They encourage a sense of playfulness and experimentation, essential components of creativity. For instance, when we feel happy, we're more likely to take creative risks, explore different solutions to a problem, or engage in divergent thinking—a way of generating multiple solutions.

Conversely, while seemingly detrimental, negative emotions can also deepen our creative expression. Feelings of sadness, anger, or frustration can lead to introspection and a deeper exploration of personal and universal themes. These emotions can drive us to create works that resonate on a profound level, offering catharsis both to the creator and the audience. For example, some of the most impactful pieces of literature, music, and art have stemmed from the artist's struggle, pain, or dissatisfaction with the status quo. In this way, negative emotions can catalyze creativity, pushing us to confront and transform our experiences into something meaningful.

Moreover, the process of creating can itself be an emotional journey. Bringing an idea to life involves frustration, exhilaration, doubt, and satisfaction. Navigating these emotional ups and downs requires resilience and a willingness to stay engaged with the work, even when it challenges us. This emotional resilience is a crucial aspect of the creative process, as it allows us to persevere through difficulties and continue refining our ideas until they reach their full expression.

The therapeutic potential of creativity as a means to process and express emotions cannot be overstated. Creative activities offer a safe outlet for exploring feelings that might be difficult to articulate in words. Whether through painting, writing, dancing, or music, creative expression provides a way to externalize our inner emotional world, giving form to what we feel and facilitating understanding and healing.

Furthermore, sharing creative work exposes our emotions to others, creating opportunities for connection and empathy. When we share stories, images, or melodies imbued with our feelings, we invite others into our emotional landscape, where they can find echoes of their experiences. This shared emotional resonance is what often makes art so powerful and moving. It bridges individual differences, reminding us of our shared humanity.

Cultivating an awareness of how our emotions influence our creativity can enhance our creative practices. By reflecting on the feelings that drive our work, we can channel them more effectively, using them as inspiration and power. This might involve consciously tapping into specific emotions during the creative process or exploring new ways to express complex feelings through our chosen medium.

To fully use the relationship between creativity and emotion, we must cultivate emotional intelligence, the capacity to identify, comprehend, and control our emotions.

Emotional intelligence helps us navigate our feelings more effectively and enriches our creative expression by allowing us to engage more deeply with our emotional experiences.

The connection between creativity and emotion is a dynamic interplay that shapes our creative endeavors and enriches our lives. Emotions fuel creativity, providing the energy and inspiration to explore, imagine, and create. At the same time, invention offers a unique avenue for expressing and understanding our emotions, fostering a deeper connection with ourselves and others. By embracing this connection, we unlock the full potential of our creative and emotional selves, discovering new ways to express the richness and complexity of the human experience.

CHAPTER 7

FOSTERING MEANINGFUL
CONNECTIONS AND RELATIONSHIPS

"We are like islands in the sea, separate on the surface but connected in the deep."

- William James

This chapter "Fostering Meaningful Connections and Relationships," dives into the essence of human connection, exploring how our relationships with others enrich our lives and contribute to our well-being. Drawing inspiration from William James' profound observation, this chapter emphasizes the invisible bonds that link us, underscoring the importance of cultivating deep, meaningful relationships. As we navigate through the complexities of life, our connections with others offer support, joy, and a sense of belonging. This chapter will lead you on an adventure to fortify current ties, forge new ones, and learn the tremendous influence of meaningful relationships on our sense of fulfillment and pleasure.

The Art of Deep Listening

Listening, genuinely listening is an art form that many of us think we practice, but few truly master. It's not just about hearing the words spoken but understanding the emotions, intentions, and unspoken messages behind them. Deep listening enhances relationships like nothing else, transforming ordinary interactions into moments of connection, empathy, and understanding. In a world where we're often distracted and only half-listening, dedicating ourselves to deep listening can revolutionize how we relate to others.

At its core, deep listening is about presence. It's about fully engaging with the person speaking, giving them your complete attention without the intention to reply but to understand. This requires setting aside your thoughts, judgments, and distractions. Imagine turning down the volume on your internal dialogue to amplify what the other person is saying. This level of attentiveness conveys respect and valuing the speaker, making them feel seen and heard.

One key to deep listening is patience. It's about allowing the other person to express themselves fully without rushing them or jumping in with your response. This may be not easy, particularly when we are having emotionally charged talks or disagreeing with what someone is saying. However, patience in listening gives space for the speaker to reveal their more profound thoughts and feelings, which are often communicated in what they don't say as much as in what they do.

Empathy is another critical aspect of deep listening. It involves trying to understand the speaker's emotions and experiences from their perspective. This doesn't mean you must agree with them; you see the world through their eyes momentarily. Empathy builds a bridge of understanding between people, fostering a sense of closeness and trust essential for strong relationships.

Asking questions is a powerful tool in deep listening. Thoughtful, open-ended questions encourage the speaker to explore and express their thoughts more fully. It shows that you're engaged and interested in understanding them better. These questions can clarify misunderstandings and reveal deeper layers of meaning, enriching the conversation and strengthening the connection.

Deep listening also involves being mindful of non-verbal cues. Much of communication is non-verbal, including body language, facial expressions, and tone of voice. Attention to these signals can give you additional insight into the speaker's emotions and intentions, often communicating more than words alone. Responding to these non-verbal cues, whether with a nod, a smile, or a sympathetic expression, can make the speaker feel genuinely heard and understood.

Moreover, deep listening extends beyond individual conversations. It's about cultivating a listening attitude in all your interactions. This means being open and curious about others' perspectives, valuing diversity of thought, and being willing to learn from everyone you encounter. By adopting this mindset, you create an environment where deep listening becomes the norm, enhancing your personal relationships and the broader community around you.

One of the most profound benefits of deep listening is its ability to heal and transform relationships. When people feel genuinely heard, it reduces conflict, builds empathy, and fosters a sense of mutual respect. Deep listening can turn misunderstandings into opportunities for growth, resentment into compassion, and distance into intimacy.

However, practicing deep listening can be challenging. It requires intention, effort, and sometimes stepping outside our comfort zone. It's a skill that needs to be cultivated and practiced regularly. But the rewards are well worth the effort. Deep listening can turn fleeting interactions into meaningful connections, acquaintances into close friends, and conflict into understanding.

In essence, mastering the art of deep listening is one of the most potent ways to enhance your relationships. It's more than just hearing words; it's about connecting with others profoundly and fostering understanding, empathy, and respect. By committing to deep listening, you enrich your life and contribute to a more compassionate, understanding world.

Vulnerability as a Strength in Connections

Embracing vulnerability in our relationships can transform how we connect with others, turning superficial interactions into deep, meaningful connections. Exposure is often considered a risk when opening up and showing our true selves, including our fears, hopes, and insecurities. However, this very openness paves the way for genuine emotional connections, fostering intimacy, trust, and understanding.

The strength of vulnerability lies in its ability to break down walls. We all wear masks and build fortresses around our hearts to protect ourselves from judgment, rejection, and hurt. But these defenses also keep us from genuinely connecting with others. By choosing to be vulnerable, we invite others to see us as we are, flaws and all. This act of courage can inspire others to lower their defenses, leading to a deeper level of mutual understanding and acceptance.

One of the first steps in embracing vulnerability is self-acceptance. Recognizing and accepting our imperfections allows us to share ourselves more openly. It's about acknowledging that we all work in progress, deserving of compassion and understanding. Taking ourselves reduces the fear of exposure often accompanying vulnerability, making it easier to share our true selves.

Creating a safe space is crucial for vulnerability to flourish. This means choosing carefully whom you open up to, ensuring they respect your feelings, listen without judgment, and reciprocate your openness. A safe space also involves setting boundaries and understanding that vulnerability does not mean sharing everything with everyone but being selective about what we share and with whom.

Effective communication plays a vital role in forming deeper connections through vulnerability. It involves sharing our thoughts and feelings and actively listening to others. Communicating in a clear, honest, and empathetic manner helps prevent misunderstandings and builds a foundation of trust. Remember, vulnerability is a two-way street that requires sharing and listening.

Vulnerability also challenges us to confront our fears of rejection and judgment. The possibility of not being accepted for who we are can be daunting. However, facing these fears is a step toward growth. It teaches us resilience and reaffirms the value of authenticity in our relationships. We often find that our fears are unfounded and that our openness leads to more robust, supportive connections.

Patience is vital when building vulnerability in relationships. Deep connections take time to happen; they require time and consistent effort. It's about gradually opening up and allowing the relationship to develop naturally. Every tiny act of vulnerability builds the relationship and opens the door to a more profound emotional exchange.

The benefits of embracing vulnerability in our connections are profound. It leads to more authentic relationships where people feel seen, heard, and valued. Exposure fosters empathy, as sharing and understanding each other's struggles and triumphs bring people closer. It also enhances emotional intimacy, creating a sense of closeness and belonging that is deeply fulfilling.

However, it's important to remember that vulnerability is not about oversharing or using openness to burden others. It's about sharing with intention and understanding that vulnerability is a gift we offer, not an obligation for others to accept. By approaching vulnerability with wisdom and discernment, we cultivate connections that are not only deeper but also healthier and more sustainable.

In essence, vulnerability is a strength at the heart of meaningful connections. It is the courage to be open about our true selves, the compassion to accept others as they are, and the wisdom to build relationships on a foundation of trust and understanding. By embracing vulnerability, we enrich our relationships and discover the true power of connection. We find genuine companionship, love, and a sense of belonging through our openness, transforming our interactions into deep, emotional relationships that nourish our souls.

Cultivating Empathy and Understanding

Cultivating empathy and understanding is akin to nurturing a garden; it requires attention, care, and the right conditions to flourish. Heart, the ability to understand and share the feelings of another, is the cornerstone of solid and meaningful relationships. It enables deeper connections with others, encouraging respect and understanding amongst them. Developing empathy involves several critical practices that, when embraced, can significantly enhance our relationships with those around us.

Firstly, actively listening is essential for empathy. It's not just about hearing words but about fully engaging with the speaker, understanding their perspective, and recognizing the emotions behind what they're saying. This means setting aside your thoughts and judgments to be present with the person sharing. Active listening demonstrates that you value their experiences and feelings, laying the groundwork for a deeper connection.

Practicing perspective-taking is another vital aspect of developing empathy. This is placing oneself in the position of another person and picturing their feelings, ideas, and experiences as though they were your own. Perspective-taking can be challenging, especially when we have different backgrounds or beliefs, but it's crucial for building empathy. It helps us understand the reasons behind others' actions and reactions, promoting a more compassionate response.

Being curious about others' experiences can also enhance empathy. When you pose open-ended inquiries and demonstrate a sincere interest in their lives, people are more willing to open up and disclose more of themselves. This curiosity deepens one's understanding of others and signals that one cares about them beyond the surface level.

Recognizing and managing one's own emotions is critical to empathetic interactions. Awareness of how one's feelings influence one's responses allows one to approach conversations with a clear, open mind. It also helps prevent one's emotions from overshadowing the other person's, ensuring that the focus remains on understanding their perspective.

Cultivating a non-judgmental attitude is crucial for empathy. Suspending judgment doesn't mean agreeing with everything someone says or does but accepting their experiences and emotions as valid. Approaching interactions with an open heart and mind fosters an environment where empathy can thrive.

Empathy can also be strengthened through shared experiences. Participating in activities or facing challenges together can create a powerful emotional bond. These shared experiences provide insight into each other's thoughts and feelings, enhancing mutual understanding.

Reflecting on your interactions can further develop empathy. Consider how you responded to others, what you learned about their perspectives, and how you might approach similar situations differently. Reflection encourages continuous learning and growth in empathetic understanding.

Finally, practicing empathy extends beyond individual relationships to how we interact with the broader community. It involves showing compassion and understanding to people from different backgrounds, cultures, and situations. We contribute to a more compassionate, understanding world by embracing empathy in all our interactions.

Developing empathy and understanding is an ongoing journey that enriches our relationships and lives. We can build stronger, more empathetic connections by actively listening, practicing perspective-taking, being curious, managing our emotions, maintaining a non-judgmental attitude, sharing experiences, and reflecting on our interactions. These practices bring us closer to those around us and help us become more compassionate and understanding individuals, capable of nurturing deep, meaningful relationships in all areas of our lives.

I am setting Boundaries for Healthier Relationships

Setting and respecting personal boundaries is a vital component of healthy relationships. Edges help us define what we are comfortable with and how we would like to be treated by others. They are essential for mutual respect and understanding, allowing us to maintain our integrity and well-being in our interactions. Here's how to navigate setting and respecting personal boundaries for healthier relationships.

Understanding what boundaries are is the first step. Boundaries can be emotional, physical, or mental limits we set to protect ourselves. Emotional boundaries relate to our feelings, physical boundaries to our personal space and touch, and mental boundaries to our thoughts and opinions. Recognizing your right to have these boundaries is crucial. Everyone deserves to feel safe and respected.

Identifying your boundaries is a personal journey. It requires introspection and reflection on past experiences. Consider situations where you felt uncomfortable, disrespected, or overwhelmed. These feelings often signal crossed boundaries. By understanding your limits, you can better articulate them to others.

The next step is communicating your boundaries clearly. It's important to express your limits straightforwardly and assertively. This doesn't mean being aggressive or confrontational. Instead, use "I" statements to describe how certain behaviors affect you and what you need instead. For example, "I feel overwhelmed when we spend every weekend together. I need some weekends to myself."

Listening to and respecting others' boundaries is as important as setting your own. Observe both spoken and nonverbal signs that convey how comfortable someone is. If someone expresses a limitation, acknowledge it and adjust your behavior accordingly. This mutual respect builds trust and strengthens relationships.

Expect some resistance. Only some people will respond positively to your boundaries. Some might test or push back against them, especially if they're not used to boundary-setting in the relationship. Stay firm and reiterate your boundaries if needed. Remember, anyone who consistently disrespects your limits may not have your best interests at heart.

Boundaries can change, and that's okay. As we grow and our situations change, our borders might too. Regularly review and adjust your limits as needed. Communicate any changes to those affected. Flexibility and open communication are vital to maintaining healthy relationships.

It's also essential to practice self-respect. Setting boundaries is an act of self-care and respect. By honoring your limits, you teach others how to treat you. This might mean making difficult decisions, such as distancing yourself from those who continually disrespect your boundaries. Remember, you are your own best advocate.

Reinforcing your boundaries is sometimes necessary. If someone continues to cross your boundaries after you've communicated them, you may need to enforce consequences. This could involve reducing contact with the person or ending the relationship in extreme cases. While this can be tough, it's essential for your well-being.

It might be challenging to set limits since many individuals fear harming or offending someone. However, setting boundaries is not about being selfish or unkind; it's about taking care of your mental and emotional health. With time and practice, setting boundaries without feeling guilty becomes easier.

Seek support if you need it. Setting and respecting boundaries can be challenging, especially in complicated relationships. If you're struggling, consider seeking help from friends, family, or a professional. They can offer guidance, perspective, and encouragement as you navigate setting boundaries.

Setting and respecting personal boundaries is essential for healthy, fulfilling relationships. It involves understanding your limits, communicating them clearly, respecting others' boundaries, and being prepared to enforce them when necessary. While it may be challenging, the effort leads to more robust, respectful relationships that contribute to our well-being. Remember, setting boundaries is a form of self-respect and an act of care for yourself and your relationships.

The Role of Forgiveness in Relationships: Navigating forgiveness for relationship healing

Forgiveness in relationships is a powerful yet often misunderstood concept. It's not about condoning hurtful behavior or forgetting that something painful happened. Instead, forgiveness is a proactive step towards healing and growth, both for the individual who forgives and the relationship affected. It's a complex process involving empathy, understanding, and a conscious decision to move past grievances for a healthier emotional state and connection.

At the heart of forgiveness lies the recognition of our shared humanity. Everyone makes mistakes. Understanding this can foster empathy, allowing us to see the situation from the other person's perspective. This doesn't justify hurtful actions but acknowledges that imperfection is part of being human. Doing so opens a pathway to empathy, a crucial ingredient for genuine forgiveness.

Forgiveness also involves addressing and processing your feelings. Hurt, anger, and betrayal are natural reactions to being wronged. Allowing yourself to feel these emotions is essential; burying them only leads to bitterness and resentment. The first step toward mending is acknowledging your feelings. Sometimes, this process might benefit from conversations with the person who hurt you, where you can express your feelings, and they can recognize your pain.

Forgiveness is a decision that frequently requires strength and maturity. It's critical to realize that reconciliation does not always follow from forgiveness. If keeping your distance from someone is best for your well-being, then you can forgive them. Forgiveness is primarily for your peace of mind—it helps release resentment's grip on your heart.

Forgiveness can lead to reconciliation and a stronger relationship, but it requires work from both parties. The person seeking forgiveness must show genuine remorse and a commitment to change. This might involve apologizing, making amends, or taking steps to ensure the hurtful behavior doesn't happen again. On the other side, the person offering forgiveness must genuinely let go of the resentment and allow their partner to prove their change.

Setting boundaries is crucial in the process of forgiveness. Forgiveness does not mean allowing harmful behaviors to continue. Setting clear boundaries communicates your needs and expectations, helping prevent future hurts. It also shows respect for yourself and the relationship, creating a foundation for healthier interactions.

Forgiveness is a process, not a one-time event. It can take time to regain hurt feelings and trust again. Be patient with yourself and the process. Healing doesn't happen overnight, and there might be setbacks. What's important is the commitment to moving forward.

The role of forgiveness in relationships is transformative. It can heal wounds, foster a deeper understanding and empathy, and strengthen individual bonds. By choosing forgiveness, you prioritize your emotional well-being and the health of your relationships. Remember, forgiveness is a gift you give yourself, a step towards freeing your heart from the weight of resentment and opening up to the possibility of a brighter, more connected future.

CHAPTER 8

"Change is the only constant in life."

– Heraclitus

In this "Embracing Change and Embracing the Unknown," delves into the heart of Life's most consistent and, often, most challenging aspect: change. Guided by the ancient wisdom of Heraclitus, this chapter explores the transformative power of welcoming change with open arms and stepping into the unknown with courage and optimism. As we navigate through the pages, we'll uncover strategies to cope with the inevitable shifts and transitions Life presents and thrive within them, recognizing that within the heart of uncertainty lies the potential for growth, discovery, and the unfolding of our most profound possibilities. This chapter invites us to reframe our relationship with change, viewing it not as a force to be feared but as a path to personal evolution and a deeper engagement with the tapestry of Life.

Navigating Life Transitions with Grace: Managing significant life changes

Transitions and changes abound in Life; some are expected, while others are surprised. These transitions can be challenging, whether it's starting a new job, moving to a different city, experiencing the loss of a loved one, or welcoming a new member into the family. However, navigating Life's significant changes with grace is possible, allowing us to grow and thrive despite uncertainty. Here's how you can manage meaningful Life changes with resilience and positivity.

First, acknowledge and accept your feelings. Change, even when positive, can evoke a mix of emotions—excitement, fear, sadness, or anxiety. Feeling a sense of loss is normal as you leave behind the familiar to embrace the unknown. Allow yourself to feel these emotions without judgment. Acknowledging your feelings is the first step toward managing them effectively.

Seek support from those around you. Friends, family members, and even professional counselors can offer the emotional support and guidance you need during times of transition. Sharing your thoughts and feelings can lighten your dynamic load and provide you with different perspectives and coping strategies. Recall that asking for help is a show of strength rather than weakness.

Stay connected to your routine as much as possible. While Life changes inevitably disrupt your way, maintaining certain aspects can provide stability and normalcy. Whether it's your weekly coffee date with a buddy, nightly reading before bed, or morning exercise, try to maintain regular routines and activities that make you happy and comfortable.

Set realistic expectations for yourself. Significant changes often come with a learning curve and an adjustment period. Be patient with yourself and set realistic expectations. It's okay to have only some of the answers or feel fully settled immediately. Permit yourself to take things one step at a time.

Focus on what you can control. During transition periods, it can feel like many things are out of your control. Focus on the aspects of the situation that you can influence. This might involve setting small, achievable goals for yourself, organizing your environment, or creating a plan to navigate through the change. Taking proactive steps can help reduce feelings of helplessness and boost your confidence.

Practice self-care. It is vital to look after your physical, mental, and emotional health while shifting. Ensure you're getting enough rest, eating well, exercising, and engaging in relaxing and rejuvenating activities. Self-care isn't selfish; it's necessary for managing stress and maintaining your health during transitions.

Look for learning opportunities. Every life transition, even the most challenging ones, offers opportunities for growth and learning. View the change as a chance to develop new skills, gain insights, and expand your horizons. Embracing a growth mindset can help you find value in the experience, making navigating it easier.

Cultivate an attitude of gratitude. Even amid change, there are always things to be grateful for. Focusing on these positives can shift your perspective and help you cope with the challenges. Whether it's appreciating the support of loved ones, the chance to start fresh, or simply the lessons learned along the way, gratitude can be a powerful tool for resilience.

Finally, remember that it's okay to let go. Part of navigating Life transitions with grace involves letting go of the past and embracing the future. This doesn't mean forgetting where you've come from but allowing yourself to move forward. Letting go frees up the emotional space you need to welcome new experiences and opportunities.

Acknowledging your emotions, getting help, sticking to a schedule, lowering your expectations, concentrating on what you can control, taking care of yourself, searching for chances to learn, developing thankfulness, and letting go are all essential parts of gracefully navigating Life's significant adjustments. Implementing these tactics to handle Life's transitions better may help you find resilience and personal development. Recall that Life's path involves changes, and how we take them affects our experiences and personalities.

The Growth Mindset in Facing Uncertainty: Cultivating a Mindset for Uncertain Times

In Life, uncertainty is as sure as the sunrise. Whether it's about our careers, relationships, or the world, facing the unknown can be daunting. On the other hand, adopting a growth mindset may turn uncertainty from a cause of anxiety to a chance for personal progress. A growth mindset is the conviction that commitment and diligence can enhance our skills and intellect, a concept made famous by psychologist Carol Dweck. It's about viewing challenges as opportunities to learn rather than insurmountable obstacles. Cultivating this mindset, especially during uncertain times, can significantly influence how we navigate the unpredictability of Life.

One of the core aspects of a growth mindset is embracing challenges. Uncertainty often brings challenges that we shouldn't have anticipated or prepared for. Instead of avoiding these challenges, a growth mindset encourages us to engage with them. It's about asking, "What can I learn from this situation?" rather than "Why is this happening to me?" This change in viewpoint can transform possible failures into insightful learning opportunities.

Another critical element is the persistence in the face of setbacks. Uncertain times are fraught with setbacks and failures. A growth mindset helps us see these not as evidence of our incapacity but as natural steps in the learning process. It teaches us that every failure is a chance to get feedback, reassess, and try again with new insights. This perseverance, which keeps us going forward even when the road is unclear, is essential for handling ambiguity.

Furthermore, a growth mindset emphasizes the power of effort. In uncertain times, the outcome of our actions can seem incredibly unpredictable. However, believing in the value of hard work and effort means understanding that progress and growth are often incremental and that every step forward counts. The effort we put into overcoming challenges and adapting to new circumstances fuels our growth and resilience.

Encouraging a love of learning is also integral to a growth mindset. Uncertainty often means venturing into the unknown, a powerful learning opportunity. Cultivating curiosity and a passion for learning can help us embrace uncertain times as a chance to expand our knowledge, skills, and understanding of the world. This love of learning can make us more adaptable and better equipped to handle whatever the future holds.

Equally important is finding inspiration in the success of others. In times of uncertainty, looking to people who have navigated similar challenges can be incredibly motivating. It's not about comparing our journey to theirs but about understanding that success, in any form, is achievable. Their stories can teach us valuable strategies and remind us that growth and achievement are possible, even in adversity.

Cultivating a growth mindset also involves developing resilience. The capacity to overcome adversity and regain stability is directly associated with a growth mentality. It's about maintaining a positive outlook, learning from experiences, and not being deterred by fear of failure. This resilience is essential in uncertain times because it enables us to overcome obstacles and emerge stronger.

To nurture a growth mindset, it's helpful to practice self-reflection. Regularly reflecting on our experiences, what we've learned, and how we've grown can reinforce a growth mindset. It helps us see our progress, understand our reactions to uncertainty, and identify areas for further development.

Finally, fostering a supportive environment is essential for cultivating a growth mindset. Surrounding ourselves with people who encourage learning, embrace challenges, and support each other can reinforce our growth mindset. This support network can provide encouragement, share insights, and help us stay motivated during uncertain times.

In essence, cultivating a growth mindset for uncertain times is about embracing challenges, persisting through setbacks, valuing effort, loving learning, finding inspiration in others, developing resilience, practicing self-reflection, and fostering a supportive environment. By adopting this mindset, we can navigate the unpredictability of Life with confidence and grace, viewing each uncertain moment not as a threat but as an opportunity to grow, learn, and thrive.

Finding Stability in Change: Creating points of stability during transitions

Navigating Life's transitions and changes can often feel like sailing in turbulent seas. While change is inevitable, finding stability amidst these fluctuations is critical to maintaining balance and well-being. Peace doesn't mean resisting change but establishing anchors that help us manage the uncertainties that transitions bring. Here's how you can create points of stability during times of change, ensuring that you can navigate Life's transitions with confidence and peace.

Firstly, establishing a routine can provide a comforting structure in the midst of change. Routines are the bedrock of our daily lives, offering predictability when everything else seems in flux. This could be as simple as maintaining regular meals, setting aside a few minutes for meditation or exercise daily, or having a nightly wind-down ritual before bed. These consistent habits don't just organize our days; they offer moments of peace and familiarity that can be deeply reassuring.

Finding stability amid upheaval also requires maintaining good connections. Strong connections with family, friends, and supportive communities provide emotional anchors to keep us grounded. Prioritizing these relationships, making time for regular check-ins, and being open about your challenges can strengthen your support network, reminding you that you're not alone in navigating these changes.

Focusing on your physical well-being is also essential during times of transition. Physical health significantly impacts our mental and emotional resilience. Regular physical activity, nutritious eating, and sufficient rest are fundamental practices that maintain our health and give us the strength to face challenges. Additionally, physical wellness activities can stabilize our routine, creating a sense of normalcy and continuity.

Cultivating mindfulness and a positive mindset can also be incredibly stabilizing. Mindfulness encourages us to live in the present, reducing worries about the future or ruminations about the past. Practices such as meditation, journaling, or simply spending time in nature can help cultivate mindfulness, allowing us to approach changes with a calmer, more centered perspective. Pairing this with a positive outlook, focusing on opportunities for growth and learning in the face of change, can transform our experience of transitions.

Another strategy is to identify and hold onto your core values. Our values are the guiding principles of our lives; they remain constant even when everything else is changing. Clarifying what truly matters to you can help you make decisions and take actions aligned with your true self, providing a sense of integrity and continuity amidst change.

Setting short-term goals can also offer stability. Long-term planning may seem daunting in times of uncertainty. Instead, focus on achievable, short-term objectives. These goals can act as stepping stones, giving you a sense of progress and accomplishment even when the bigger picture might be unclear.

Cultivating thankfulness may help you find stability amid change. Regularly reflecting on what you're thankful for can shift your focus from what you're losing or what's uncertain to what remains good and constant in your Life. This practice can anchor you to the present and the positive aspects of your Life, providing a stable point of emotional well-being.

Lastly, embracing change as a constant can paradoxically provide stability. Accepting that change is a natural part of Life allows us to let go of resistance and approach transitions with flexibility and openness. This acceptance doesn't happen overnight, but cultivating it can change our relationship with change, making it less daunting and more integrated into our lives.

Finding stability in change involves:

- Establishing routines.
- Nurturing relationships.
- Taking care of your physical well-being.
- Cultivating mindfulness and a positive mindset.
- Holding onto core values.
- Setting short-term goals.
- Practicing gratitude.
- Accepting change as a constant.

By implementing these strategies, you can create points of stability that help you navigate Life's transitions more smoothly and confidently. Remember, strength isn't about having a life free from change but about finding your equilibrium within the changes, ensuring that you remain grounded as you move through Life's inevitable shifts.

I am embracing the Lessons of Change: Learning and growing from Life's changes

Life's changes, whether anticipated or unexpected, are ripe with lessons. Embracing these lessons allows us to navigate change and grow from it. Every shift in our circumstances, every new challenge or opportunity, holds the potential for personal development. Learning and growing from Life's changes involve a conscious decision to look beyond the discomfort of the unfamiliar and to seek the insights and growth that change can bring.

When we encounter change, our first reactions might be resistance or fear. This is natural; change disrupts our sense of security and forces us out of our comfort zones. However, once we move past initial reactions, we can start to see change as an opportunity for learning. This shift in perspective is crucial. It transforms change from something that happens to us into something we can engage with actively and learn from.

One of the most critical lessons change teaches us is resilience. Navigating through change, especially when challenging, builds our ability to withstand adversity. We learn that we can endure much more than we thought, becoming more robust and adaptable on the other side. This resilience doesn't erase the difficulty of change but gives us confidence in our ability to handle future challenges.

Change also offers a powerful lesson in flexibility and adaptability. It teaches us that clinging too tightly to plans or expectations can lead to disappointment and frustration. Conversely, there may be unanticipated chances and successful routes if we are open to changing directions, attempting novel strategies, and being prepared to absorb the lessons from our mistakes. This flexibility helps us navigate change more effectively and opens us up to new experiences and ways of thinking.

Furthermore, change forces us to reevaluate our priorities and values. When faced with significant changes, we often have to make choices that reflect what's truly important to us. This reflection and decision-making process can clarify our values and ensure that our lives are aligned with them. It's an invitation to live more authentically, making choices that reflect our true selves.

Another lesson from change is the importance of being present. Change shakes us out of autopilot, making us more aware of the here and now. This increased consciousness can result in a greater appreciation for Life's small joys and teach us to be content and thankful despite hardship.

Change also teaches us about the power of letting go. We often live Life to release old patterns, behaviors, or relationships that no longer serve us and embrace new opportunities. Though letting go can be painful, it's also liberating. It frees up space for further growth and allows us to move forward with less baggage.

Moreover, change is a teacher of patience. Many changes yield little results and require time to unfold. Learning to be patient, trust the process, and give ourselves and others grace during times of transition is invaluable. Patience helps us approach change with a sense of calm and perseverance, knowing that growth and outcomes can't be rushed.

Lastly, embracing change teaches us humility. It reminds us that we don't have all the answers and that there's always room to learn and grow. This humility opens us up to new learning opportunities, deepens our empathy for others going through similar experiences, and keeps us grounded.

In essence, embracing the lessons of change is about seeing change not as a threat but as a teacher. It's an opportunity to learn resilience, flexibility, the value of being present, the necessity of letting go, the virtue of patience, and the humility to know we're constantly growing. By actively seeking the lessons in each change we encounter, we can navigate Life's transitions gracefully and turn them into opportunities for personal development and growth.

Developing Adaptability and Flexibility: Ski Life thrives in changing circumstances

Adaptability and flexibility Are Crucial skills for thriving in our ever-changing world. These abilities allow us to navigate Life's twists and turns with resilience, maintaining our well-being and pursuing our goals even when circumstances shift unexpectedly. Developing life skills involves a combination of mindset shifts, practical strategies, and a commitment to continuous learning and growth.

The first step in being adaptable and flexible is, first and foremost, developing a development mentality. This entails seeing difficulties as opportunities to create and learn rather than insurmountable barriers. When we believe that our abilities and intelligence can be developed through effort, good strategies, and input from others, we become more open to change and better equipped to adapt.

Practicing mindfulness is another crucial strategy. Mindfulness helps us stay present and aware, making it easier to notice when changes occur and respond more effectively. It also reduces the stress and anxiety that often accompany uncertainty, allowing us to approach differences more clearly.

Cultivating curiosity is essential for adaptability and flexibility. Being genuinely interested in new experiences, ideas, and perspectives encourages us to explore and experiment, even when unsure of the outcome. This curiosity can lead to discovering new solutions and approaches we wouldn't have considered otherwise.

Strengthening our problem-solving skills is also vital. Change often presents us with new problems to solve. We can tackle these challenges more effectively by developing strong analytical and creative thinking skills. This involves looking at issues from different angles, brainstorming multiple solutions, and being willing to experiment until we find what works.

Building a support network is crucial for thriving in changing circumstances. Surrounding ourselves with supportive people who encourage our adaptability and are willing to offer advice, feedback, and different perspectives can make navigating change much more accessible. This network can include friends, family, mentors, and colleagues.

Learning to let go of control is another crucial aspect of developing adaptability and flexibility. While it's natural to want to control our environment and outcomes, many aspects of Life are beyond our control. Accepting this can reduce frustration and help us focus on what we can influence.

Practicing resilience is closely linked to adaptability and flexibility. The capacity to overcome obstacles and carry on in the face of failures is known as resilience. Developing resilience involves:

- Focusing on our strengths.
- Learning from failures.
- Maintaining a positive outlook even in the face of adversity.

Finally, committing to lifelong learning is essential for adaptability and flexibility. The world constantly changes, and new challenges require new knowledge and skills. By staying curious and committed to education, we can ensure that we're always prepared to adapt to whatever comes our way.

Developing adaptability and flexibility is about cultivating a growth mindset, practicing mindfulness, staying curious, honing our problem-solving skills, building a supportive network, letting go of the need for control, practicing resilience, and committing to lifelong learning. By embracing these strategies, we can enhance our ability to thrive in changing circumstances, turning challenges into opportunities for growth and success.

CHAPTER 9

CULTIVATING GRATITUDE AND FINDING JOY IN EVERYDAY MOMENTS

"In ordinary life, we hardly realize that we receive a great deal more than we give, and that it is only with gratitude that life becomes rich."

- Dietrich Bonhoeffer

This chapter "Cultivating Gratitude and Finding Joy in Everyday Moments," explores gratitude's profound simplicity and transformative power. Inspired by the insightful words of Dietrich Bonhoeffer, this chapter delves into how recognizing and appreciating the abundance in our everyday lives can enrich our existence. We embark on a journey to uncover the beauty in the mundane, the extraordinary in the ordinary, and the joy in the simplest moments. Through practical advice and reflective exercises, we learn to cultivate gratitude that elevates our lives and positively impacts those around us. This chapter invites us to pause, reflect, and embrace daily life's countless gifts, teaching us to live with a fuller, more appreciative heart.

Gratitude Practices for Daily Life: Practices to cultivate gratitude.

Incorporating gratitude into daily life transforms our perspective, fostering a sense of contentment and joy even amidst challenges. Gratitude, appreciation, and gratitude for the good in our lives can significantly enhance our well-being. Here's a guide to embedding gratitude practices into your daily routine, helping you cultivate a more profound sense of gratitude.

Begin by designating a certain period every day for thankfulness. This could be in the morning as you start your day, during lunch as a midday reflection, or at night before bed. The key is consistency. By including appreciation on a daily basis, you may change your perspective from what's missing in your life to what's abundant.

Keeping a gratitude journal is one of the most effective practices. Each day, write down three things you're grateful for. These don't have to be monumental; even simple pleasures or small victories count. It could be as straightforward as a delicious meal, a kind word from a friend, or the comfort of your home. Over time, this practice highlights the positive aspects of your life and trains your mind to spot them more easily.

Expressing gratitude to others enriches your relationships and spreads positivity. Take the time to thank people who make a difference in your day, whether it's a family member, a colleague, or even a stranger. This could be through a thank-you note, a message, or verbally expressing your appreciation. Acknowledging others' roles strengthens connections and fosters a sense of community.

Incorporating gratitude into meditation or prayer can deepen the practice. Reflecting on what you're grateful for during these moments of quiet and reflection can enhance feelings of gratitude. You can focus on different aspects of your life, from personal achievements to loved ones, and feel gratitude.

Practicing mindfulness helps us live in the present moment, making recognizing and appreciating the beauty in our everyday lives easier. Simple acts like savoring your morning coffee, enjoying the sun's warmth, or listening to a favorite song can become opportunities for gratitude. Mindfulness encourages us to slow down and appreciate the now, fostering a more profound sense of thankfulness.

Sharing gratitude with a friend or family can also be a powerful practice. This could involve transferring what you're grateful for with each other or even starting a gratitude challenge, where you share daily messages of gratitude. This shared practice amplifies your appreciation and helps build a positive and supportive environment around you.

Visual reminders can also serve as cues to practice gratitude. Keeping inspirational quotes, photos of loved ones, or symbols of what you're grateful for in your workspace or home can remind you to take a moment and reflect on your blessings. These visual cues can serve as anchors, bringing your focus back to gratitude throughout the day.

Lastly, volunteering and acts of kindness are profound expressions of gratitude. One way to share your appreciation for what you have is to give back to the community or assist someone in need. These acts reinforce our interconnectedness and the importance of supporting one another, amplifying feelings of gratitude and fulfillment.

In essence, cultivating gratitude daily is about recognizing the abundance around us and within us. It involves acknowledging the good, expressing thanks, and giving back. By embedding gratitude practices into our routines, we can transform our outlook, enhance our well-being, and foster deeper connections with those around us. Gratitude turns what we have into enough and more, teaching us to find joy and contentment in the present moment.

Recognizing Joy in the Ordinary: Appreciating Simple Pleasures.

Finding joy in the ordinary is an art that transforms our daily lives into a series of moments worth savoring. It's about appreciating the simple pleasures that often go unnoticed when we're caught up in everyday life's hustle and bustle. This practice can significantly enhance our sense of happiness and contentment, grounding us in the present and reminding us of the beauty in the world around us.

The first step in recognizing joy in the ordinary is to slow down. Our fast-paced lifestyles can easily cause us to lose sight of the little things that make us happy. By intentionally slowing down, we allow ourselves the space to notice and appreciate these moments. Whether it's taking a few extra minutes to enjoy your morning coffee, walking a bit slower to take in your surroundings, or simply pausing to breathe deeply, slowing down is essential for appreciating the beauty in everyday life.

Paying attention to your senses is another way to find joy in the ordinary. Each purpose offers a unique pathway to pleasure and appreciation. Listen to the sound of rain on the roof, savor the taste of a home-cooked meal, feel the sun's warmth on your skin, inhale the scent of fresh flowers, and observe the beauty of a sunset. Using your senses allows you to appreciate small moments and stay in the present.

Mindfulness practices can also improve one's capacity to find joy in the mundane. To practice mindfulness, one must be present, involved, and judgment-free in the present moment. Practicing mindfulness increases one's awareness of one's surroundings and experiences, making it possible to discover delight in things one might otherwise pass by.

Gratitude plays a crucial role in appreciating simple pleasures. Concentrating on your thankfulness automatically makes you more aware of the good things in your life, such as the happiness that may be found in everyday moments. Make it a habit to reflect on what you're grateful for each day, whether it's a kind gesture from a friend, the comfort of your home, or the beauty of nature.

Creating rituals around everyday activities can also help you find joy in the ordinary. Adding elements of pleasure or mindfulness can transform mundane tasks into enjoyable opportunities. For example, you could light a candle and play your favorite music while you cook dinner or turn your morning shower into a moment of relaxation and reflection.

Sharing simple pleasures with others can amplify the joy they bring. The shared experience of laughter, conversation, or a shared meal can deepen relationships and make ordinary moments more memorable and enjoyable. The presence of loved ones can transform simple pleasures into cherished memories.

Finally, adopting a curious and open attitude can lead you to discover joy in unexpected places. Approach the world with wonder and openness, and you'll find that even ordinary experiences can offer new insights, delights, and reasons to smile.

Recognizing joy in the ordinary is about embracing the moment, engaging your senses, practicing gratitude, and sharing experiences with others. It reminds us that happiness often lies in the simplest things, waiting to be noticed and appreciated. By cultivating an awareness of the simple pleasures surrounding us, we can enrich our lives with moments of joy every day.

The Ripple Effect of Gratitude and Joy: How gratitude and joy impact others

Joy and gratitude aren't only internal feelings; they can impact lives far beyond our own. Like stones tossed into a pond, acts of gratitude and joy can spread outwards, profoundly impacting those around us. This ripple effect can transform relationships, foster positive environments, and influence the wider community.

When we express gratitude, whether through a simple thank you, a thoughtful note, or a kind gesture, it acknowledges the value and effort of others. This recognition can significantly boost the recipient's mood and self-esteem, making them feel appreciated and valued. This positive feeling often encourages them to extend kindness and gratitude towards others, perpetuating a cycle of positivity.

Moreover, joy and gratitude have contagious qualities. Just as laughter can spread through a room, so can expressions of joy and gratitude. Sharing our happiness or gratitude with others can uplift their spirits and inspire them to find joy and appreciation in their own lives. This shared positivity can strengthen individual bonds, creating a more supportive and connected community.

Gratitude and joy also can change the tone of interactions and environments. For example, a culture of appreciation can lead to increased job satisfaction, better teamwork, and higher productivity in workplaces. Workers are more likely to be engaged and driven if they feel valued and appreciated. Similarly, in family and social settings, expressions of gratitude and joy can create a more harmonious and loving atmosphere, making it easier to navigate conflicts and build stronger relationships.

Furthermore, happiness and appreciation have a contagious impact that might increase people's empathy and understanding of one another. Seeing others expressing thankfulness and joy, especially in challenging situations, can inspire us to adopt a more compassionate and empathetic perspective. This can break down barriers, foster mutual understanding, and encourage acts of kindness and support within the community.

The impact of gratitude and joy also extends to our overall well-being. Studies have shown that practicing gratitude and focusing on pleasure can improve mental and physical health, reduce stress, and increase resilience. These benefits enhance our quality of life and enable us to be more present and supportive of others. We can favorably influence others around us when we are well and happy.

In essence, the ripple effect of gratitude and joy underscores the interconnectedness of our experiences and well-being. By consciously practicing gratitude and seeking joy, we enrich our lives and contribute to a more positive, supportive, and joyful world. These seemingly small acts and expressions can have far-reaching effects, creating waves of positivity that touch the lives of many. In this way, gratitude and joy are personal virtues and powerful forces for collective good.

The Connection Between Gratitude and Well-being: Exploring the health benefits of gratitude

The connection between gratitude and well-being is a fascinating interplay that underscores the profound impact of a thankful disposition on our overall health. Rooted in countless studies and personal testimonies, the health benefits of gratitude stretch across the physical, mental, and emotional spectrums, offering a simple yet powerful approach to enhancing our quality of life.

At the heart of this connection is the concept that gratitude shifts our focus from what's lacking to what's abundant in our lives. This shift in perspective can significantly influence our mental health. Regular gratitude practice has been linked to a decrease in feelings of depression and anxiety. It fosters a positive mindset, helping us cope with stress and adversity more effectively. By acknowledging and appreciating the good, we buffer ourselves against negative thoughts and feelings, creating a more optimistic outlook.

Gratitude also plays a crucial role in enhancing our physical health. Studies suggest that individuals who engage in gratitude report fewer physical symptoms, experience better sleep, and may even have more robust immune systems. Being thankful can encourage healthier lifestyle choices, such as exercising regularly and making better dietary choices. Moreover, the stress-reducing effects of gratitude can directly impact physical health, given the well-documented link between stress and various health issues.

Social well-being is another area where gratitude casts its positive ripple. Expressing gratitude can strengthen relationships by fostering a sense of closeness and appreciation between people. It increases our propensity to act prosocial, such as lending a hand to others and strengthening our sense of connection and belonging. These strong social bonds are fundamental to our emotional well-being and can provide critical support during challenging times.

Gratitude can also improve our emotional well-being by enhancing our ability to savor positive experiences. By taking the time to appreciate the good moments, we deepen our enjoyment and satisfaction with life. This practice can help build emotional resilience, equipping us with the inner resources to face life's ups and downs with a more balanced and grounded approach.

Interestingly, gratitude has a bidirectional relationship with well-being; not only does appreciation contribute to well-being, but experiencing well-being can also foster a sense of gratitude. This good cycle creates a positive feedback loop where appreciation and wellness reinforce and enhance each other.

Incorporating gratitude into our lives doesn't require grand gestures. Well-being can profoundly affect our well-being, such as maintaining a gratitude journal, reflecting on things we're thankful for daily, or expressing appreciation to others. These practices help anchor us in the present moment, encouraging a fuller, more appreciative engagement with well-being essence; the connection between gratitude and well-being is profound and far-reaching. Appreciation acts as a catalyst for positive change, enhancing our mental well-being and emotional health. It encourages us to appreciate the present, strengthens our relationships, and builds a foundation for resilience and happiness. Embracing gratitude improves our lives and contributes to a more positive, connected world.

I am creating a Gratitude Mindset: Strategies for developing a grateful outlook

Developing a gratitude mindset transforms how we perceive and interact with the world. It's about cultivating an attitude that appreciates the present and finds the silver lining, even in less ideal circumstances. Here are strategies to nurture a grateful outlook on life, turning gratitude into a habitual way of seeing and being.

Practice Mindfulness

Mindfulness is the foundation of a gratitude mindset. By being fully present and engaged at the moment, we're more likely to notice and appreciate the beauty and goodness around us. Mindfulness practices, such as meditation, prayer and/or simply paying attention to our surroundings without judgment, can heighten our awareness of life's blessings.

Keep a Gratitude Journal

One of the best methods to promote thankfulness is to keep a gratitude notebook. Daily, jot down three to five things you're thankful for. These don't have to be grand or extraordinary; simple, everyday joys often contribute most to our sense of happiness. Regularly reflecting on these positives can shift your focus from what's missing to what's abundant in your life.

Set Reminders

Amidst the everyday chaos, it might be simple to overlook taking a moment to acknowledge and be grateful. Setting reminders on your phone or posting sticky notes in places you frequently look at can prompt you to reflect on something you're thankful for. These small nudges can help integrate gratitude more seamlessly into your daily routine.

Express Gratitude to Others

Expressing gratitude to others brightens their day and reinforces your sense of gratitude. Make it a habit to thank people for specific acts of kindness or simply being in your life. This practice strengthens relationships and creates a positive feedback loop of appreciation and joy.

Reframe Challenges

Gratitude isn't just about celebrating the good times; it's also about finding something to be grateful for in challenges. Every difficulty carries a lesson or an opportunity for growth. Reframing setbacks as chances to learn and develop, you cultivate resilience and a more nuanced, grateful perspective.

Volunteer and Give Back

Participating in community service or lending a hand to people in need will make you feel more grateful. Acts of service offer perspective, reminding us of what we have and the power of generosity. The fulfillment from making a positive difference in someone's life can significantly boost gratitude.

Expand Your Gratitude Practice

Gratitude can extend beyond personal reflection; it can be woven into various aspects of your life. Incorporate gratitude into your family dinners by sharing what each person is thankful for, or start meetings with a moment of appreciation. These practices can spread gratitude, creating a more positive, appreciative environment for everyone involved.

Embrace Gratitude in Tough Times

Graduation can be most potent during our most challenging moments. Finding even the most minor thing to be grateful for amidst adversity can be incredibly grounding. It's not about denying the pain or difficulty but finding a glimmer of hope or joy amidst the darkness.

Be Patient with Yourself

Cultivating a gratitude mindset is a journey, not a destination. There will be days when feeling thankful comes easily and days when it feels nearly impossible. Be patient and gentle with yourself. The goal isn't perfection but progress towards a more grateful, joyful way of living.

Creating a gratitude mindset involves intentional practices and a willingness to see the world through a lens of appreciation. It's about recognizing the value in every moment and every experience, embracing gratitude not just as an occasional practice but as a fundamental aspect of your outlook on life. Using these techniques, you may cultivate a lasting and profound sense of thankfulness that will improve your well-being and how you interact with the outside world.

CHAPTER 10

"Love cannot remain by itself—it has no meaning. Love has to be put into action, and that action is service."

- Mother Teresa

This chapter invites readers to explore the transformative impact of love when it transcends words and becomes an active force for good in the world. It delves into how service to others enriches the lives of those we help and deepens our experience of love, fostering personal growth and a more profound sense of connection with the broader tapestry of humanity. Through stories, insights, and practical guidance, this chapter illuminates the path to living a life marked by compassionate action, encouraging us to embrace love as a powerful catalyst for positive change.

The Transformative Power of Giving: How giving enriches the giver and receiver

In its many forms, giving carries a transformative power that extends far beyond the act itself. It's a fundamental expression of human kindness that enriches both the giver and the receiver, weaving a fabric of connection and compassion that strengthens communities and fosters mutual understanding. This dynamic interaction provides immediate help or joy to the receiver and imparts profound emotional and psychological benefits to the giver, highlighting the reciprocal nature of giving.

At the heart of giving is the concept of altruism, the selfless concern for the well-being of others. Selfless acts, ranging from donating to charities and volunteering time to simple gestures of kindness, embody the essence of giving without the expectation of reward. However, the act of giving itself activates a rewarding process, one that benefits the giver in numerous ways.

Giving can evoke feelings of happiness and satisfaction for the giver, a phenomenon often referred to as the "helper's high." This sense of joy stems from releasing endorphins, natural mood lifters. Engaging in acts of generosity has been linked to increased well-being, reduced stress levels, and a greater sense of purpose and fulfillment. It underscores the idea that in giving, we find a deeper connection to our humanity and a broader understanding of belonging to a community or a cause greater than ourselves.

Furthermore, giving promotes gratitude and appreciation. When we give, we often gain a new perspective on our circumstances, fostering a sense of appreciation for what we have. This change in viewpoint can result in a happier and more grateful attitude towards improving our general well-being.

The impact of giving extends to the receiver, who benefits from the tangible aid or kindness received and the knowledge that someone cares. This sense of being cared for can significantly affect the receiver's emotional and mental health, offering hope, reducing feelings of isolation, and fostering a sense of connection and community. Receiving can inspire recipients to pay it forward, perpetuating a cycle of generosity and kindness.

Giving also plays a crucial role in building and strengthening relationships. Kindness and generosity create bonds of trust and mutual respect, laying the foundation for deeper connections. In giving, we communicate empathy, compassion, and a willingness to support others, which are critical components of healthy and supportive relationships.

Moreover, giving has the power to create positive ripple effects within communities. A single act of kindness can inspire others to engage in similar acts, multiplying the impact and fostering a culture of generosity and Support. This collective action can address broader social issues, improve community well-being, and bring significant positive change.

In essence, the transformative power of giving lies in its ability to enrich both the giver and the receiver, creating a cycle of generosity that fosters well-being, gratitude, and connection. We can contribute to a more compassionate, supportive, and connected world by embracing giving as a fundamental part of our lives. In all its forms, sharing is a testament to the profound impact of kindness and generosity on individuals and communities.

Love as an Action: Practical ways to show love through service

Serving others is a way to demonstrate love by converting emotions into practical deeds that improve the lives of others. It's a powerful way to express love, moving beyond words to demonstrate care, Support, and commitment. Here are practical ways to show love through service, fostering deeper connections, and making a meaningful difference in the lives of those around you.

Listen Actively

One of the most profound ways to serve others is by offering your undivided attention. Active listening goes beyond just hearing words; it's about understanding the message, empathizing, and responding thoughtfully. It shows that you value the other person's thoughts and feelings, creating a space where they feel seen and heard.

Acts of Kindness

Simple acts of kindness can be powerful expressions of love. This might include cooking a meal for someone going through a tough time, helping a neighbor with yard work, or offering errands for an overwhelmed friend. Though seemingly small, these actions can significantly impact someone's day, making them feel cared for and supported.

Volunteer Together

Volunteering for essential causes or organizations for you or your loved ones is a meaningful way to show love through service. It provides assistance to those in need and strengthens your bond with your loved ones as you work towards a common goal, sharing experiences that embody compassion and altruism.

Be Present in Times of Need

Sometimes, the best way to show love is simply by being there for someone in their time of need. Whether offering a shoulder to cry on, being present during a difficult period, or providing practical Support during challenging times, your presence can offer immense comfort and assurance.

Offer Words of Encouragement

Encouraging words can be a service, uplifting someone's spirits and helping them see their strength and potential. Whether through a heartfelt letter, a motivational text, or a sincere compliment, showing your belief in someone's abilities can inspire them to persevere and strive for their goals.

Teach and Share Knowledge

Sharing your knowledge and skills with others is a generous way to serve. Whether it's tutoring a student, teaching a friend a new skill, or sharing your professional expertise with someone looking to grow in their career, these acts of service can have a lasting impact on someone's life.

Practice Patience

Sometimes, serving others requires Patience, especially when dealing with challenging situations or differences of opinion. Practicing Patience, offering understanding instead of judgment, and working through disagreements with compassion are powerful ways to show love and respect.

Support Personal Growth

Encouraging and supporting the personal growth of those you care about is a profound act of service. This might involve supporting their hobbies, cheering on their new ventures, or offering constructive feedback. It's about wanting the best for them and helping them achieve their dreams.

Perform Unexpected Acts of Service

Surprising someone with an act of service can be a delightful way to show love. This could be anything from cleaning up the house to taking care of a chore they dislike or planning a surprise outing. These unexpected gestures can bring joy and show that you think of them and their well-being.

Incorporating love as an action into daily life strengthens relationships, builds a sense of community, and enriches our lives. By showing love through service, we support and uplift those around us and cultivate a more profound understanding of connection and purpose. When expressed as service, love becomes a transformative force that can change lives, including ours.

Balancing Self-love with Service to Others: Finding equilibrium between self-care and serving

Finding a balance between self-love and service to others is akin to walking a tightrope, where leaning too far in one direction can lead to falling. Both are integral to a fulfilling life; self-love ensures our well-being while serving others and connects us to the broader tapestry of human experience. The key is to cultivate equilibrium, ensuring that caring for oneself fuels our ability to serve others and that serving others enriches our lives without leading to burnout. Here's how to navigate this delicate balance, nurturing a life that honors both self-care and the commitment to serve.

Understand the Value of Self-Love

Recognize that self-love is not selfish; it's essential. It is the cornerstone upon which we construct our ability to assist others. Self-love guarantees that you are in a strong and healthy position, allowing you to give to others more efficiently, just like the safety guidelines on an airline suggest putting on your oxygen mask before aiding others. It entails taking good care of your mental, emotional, and physical well-being and establishing limits to safeguard your energy.

Set Healthy Boundaries

Boundaries are crucial in balancing self-love with service. They help define how much you can give without depleting yourself. Setting and communicating clear boundaries with those you serve and even with yourself ensures that you can continue to help others without sacrificing your well-being. It's about knowing when to say yes and when to say no, ensuring that your acts of service are sustainable.

Practice Mindful Service

Engage in service mindfully, choosing activities that resonate with your values and interests. This alignment ensures that serving others is also nourishing for you, turning it into a source of joy and fulfillment rather than an obligation that drains your energy. When service aligns with your passions, it doesn't feel like a chore; instead, it becomes another expression of self-love.

Prioritize Self-Care

Make self-care a priority, scheduling it just like any other important activity. Whether through exercise, meditation, hobbies, or rest, self-care practices are non-negotiable for maintaining the equilibrium between self-love and service. Regular self-care replenishes your energy and enhances your effectiveness and joy in serving others.

Reflect and Reassess Regularly

Regularly reflect on how well your balancing self-love and service. Ask yourself if your current practices are sustainable and fulfilling or if you feel stretched too thin. Be honest in your assessment and willing to make changes if necessary. This ongoing reflection helps you stay attuned to your needs and adjust your commitments to prevent burnout.

Learn to Receive

Balance is not just about giving; it's also about being open to receiving. Allowing others to help you, accepting gratitude, and recognizing the impact of your service can replenish your spirit. It reinforces the cycle of giving and receiving that underpins healthy relationships and communities.

Cultivate gratitude

Gratitude can bridge self-love and service, enhancing joy and fulfillment. Practicing gratitude for the opportunity to serve, the capabilities that allow you to help others, and the blessings in your own life can deepen your sense of purpose and connection.

Seek Support

Remember that you don't have to do it all alone. Seeking Support from friends, family, or community resources can lighten your load, allowing you to serve more effectively while caring for yourself. Talking to others about your experiences might give you a different viewpoint, Support, and helpful advice.

Balancing self-love with service to others requires intention, awareness, and the courage to prioritize your well-being alongside your desire to help. By cultivating this balance, you ensure that your acts of service are sustainable and joy-filled, contributing positively to your life and those you aim to serve. This equilibrium not only fosters personal growth but also amplifies the impact of your service, creating ripples of positivity and Support that extend far beyond the immediate acts of kindness.

The Impact of Service on Community: Understanding how acts of service benefit the wider community

The impact of service on a community is profound and multifaceted, extending far beyond the immediate effects of individual acts of kindness or volunteer work. Service acts as a powerful catalyst for positive change, fostering a sense of unity, strengthening social bonds, and improving the quality of life for everyone involved. Here's a closer look at how acts of service benefit the wider community.

Fosters a Sense of Belonging and Unity

Service brings people together, creating a sense of belonging and unity. Acts of compassion by individuals contribute to a group effort for the betterment of society. This shared purpose can break down barriers, bridging gaps between a community's different social, economic, and cultural groups. The collaboration and camaraderie developed through service projects reinforce the idea that we are all part of a larger community, working towards shared goals.

Strengthens Social Bonds

Acts of service strengthen social bonds by building trust and reciprocity among community members. When people come together to help one another, they lay the foundation for more robust, supportive relationships. These connections are crucial in times of need, creating a safety net that individuals can rely on. Furthermore, service promotes empathy and understanding, often involving stepping into someone else's shoes and seeing the world from their perspective.

Enhances Well-being

Service has a significant positive impact on the well-being of both the giver and receiver; for those who serve, engaging in philanthropic activities has increased happiness, reduced stress, and even improved physical health. The assistance recipients receive can alleviate hardships, enhance their quality of life, and offer hope. Moreover, witnessing acts of kindness can inspire others to act, creating positivity throughout the community.

Addresses Community Needs

Service directly benefits the community by addressing specific needs and challenges. Whether through organized volunteer programs or individual acts of kindness, service efforts can fill gaps, provide essential resources, and improve community facilities. From tutoring and mentoring programs that support education to environmental cleanup projects that protect local ecosystems, service initiatives can make a tangible difference in the quality of life within a community.

Empowers Individuals

Engaging in service empowers individuals by giving them a sense of agency and purpose. Participants in community service initiatives frequently acquire new abilities, priceless experience, and confidence. This empowerment can inspire further involvement in civic activities, leadership roles, and other initiatives that contribute to community development.

Promotes Social Justice

Service can also be a vehicle for promoting social justice and equity within communities. By addressing systemic issues such as poverty, education inequality, and access to healthcare, service projects can help level the playing field and create more equitable opportunities for all community members. In doing so, service acts as a force for social change, challenging injustices and advocating for the rights and well-being of underserved populations.

Cultivates a Culture of Generosity

Finally, acts of service cultivate a culture of generosity and compassion within communities. As people witness and participate in acts of kindness and volunteerism, these values become woven into the fabric of the community. This culture of generosity encourages ongoing involvement in service activities, ensuring that the community continues to thrive and support its members.

In essence, the impact of service on a community is profound, with benefits that ripple out to touch every aspect of community life. From fostering unity and strengthening social bonds to addressing specific needs and promoting social justice, acts of service create healthier, more vibrant communities where individuals feel connected, supported, and empowered to make a difference.

Leading with Love in Difficult Times

Leading with love and compassion during difficult times is an ethical choice and a powerful strategy for navigating challenges with grace and resilience. Compassionate leadership becomes crucial in a family, community, or organizational context when facing uncertainty, crisis, or change. It involves prioritizing empathy, understanding, and care in interactions and decisions, recognizing that how we lead impacts outcomes and the well-being of those we lead.

Empathy as a Foundation

Empathy is at the core of leading with love—the ability to understand and share another's feelings. Empathetic leadership means truly listening to the concerns, fears, and hopes of those affected by difficult times. It requires being present, showing genuine interest, and responding with sensitivity to the emotional states of others. This approach fosters trust and safety, creating an environment where people feel supported and valued.

Communication with Compassion

Transparent and compassionate communication is vital during challenging periods. Leaders must convey messages honestly and sensitively, ensuring precise and carefully delivered information. This includes acknowledging the difficulty of the situation, sharing what is known and what isn't, and expressing commitment to navigating the challenges together. Compassionate communication can alleviate anxiety and build a shared sense of purpose and direction.

Flexibility and Understanding

Difficult times often call for flexibility in policies, expectations, and deadlines. Leading with love means recognizing individuals' unique challenges and adapting to meet those needs. It might involve offering additional Support, modifying workloads, or providing resources to help navigate personal and professional demands. Flexibility demonstrates understanding and prioritizes the human aspect of leadership.

Fostering a Supportive Community

Leadership with love and compassion fosters a sense of community and mutual Support. By encouraging collaboration, offering opportunities for connection, and facilitating peer support, leaders can strengthen the social bonds critical for resilience. A supportive community helps individuals cope with stress and harnesses the collective strength and creativity needed to overcome challenges.

Modeling Self-care and Encouraging Well-being

Compassionate leaders recognize the importance of self-care and well-being for themselves and those they lead. Modeling healthy behaviors, such as taking breaks, seeking Support, and setting boundaries, can encourage others to prioritize their well-being. Leaders can also promote well-being by providing resources and creating policies that support mental and physical health.

Acting with Integrity and Purpose

Leading with love during difficult times means making decisions with integrity, guided by a clear sense of purpose and values. It's about doing what's right, not just what's easy or practical. This commitment to ethical leadership, even when faced with tough choices, inspires trust and respect, reinforcing the leader's role as a moral compass for the community or organization.

Empowering and Inspiring Hope

Finally, leading with love is about empowering others and inspiring hope. It involves highlighting strengths, acknowledging progress, and envisioning the future. Compassionate leaders can inspire hope and motivate action by focusing on possibilities and affirming the collective ability to navigate through challenges.

Leading with love and compassion in difficult times is a holistic approach that emphasizes empathy, supportive communication, flexibility, community, well-being, integrity, and hope. It acknowledges the complexities of human experiences during challenges and seeks to navigate them with kindness, understanding, and a deep commitment to the well-being of all involved. Such leadership helps us weather the storm and emerge more robust, connected, and resilient.

Service as a Path to Personal Growth

Service to others is not just an altruistic act meant to benefit the recipient; it's also a profound avenue for personal growth and a deeper sense of purpose. Engaging in acts of service allows us to step outside ourselves, connect with the broader world, and contribute to something larger than our individual lives. This process of giving and connecting enriches us, offering lessons in empathy, humility, and gratitude and fostering a sense of fulfillment that is deeply intertwined with personal development.

Enhances Empathy and Compassion

Service puts us directly in touch with others' needs and challenges, fostering a deep sense of empathy and compassion. By witnessing the struggles and successes of those we help, we develop a more nuanced understanding of the human experience. This empathy makes us more effective in our service and enriches our personal relationships and our broader view of the world.

Builds a Sense of Connection and Community

Serving others reinforces the idea that we are all interconnected. It breaks down barriers of isolation and builds bridges of understanding and Support. Through service, we become part of a community of givers bound by the shared goal of making a positive impact. This sense of belonging and collective purpose can be incredibly fulfilling, countering the individualism that often defines modern life.

Fosters Personal Resilience

The challenges inherent in service push us out of our comfort zones, testing our limits and teaching us about our capacities for adaptability and resilience. Whether navigating the complexities of volunteer work, facing the emotional intensity of helping those in need, or simply persisting in the face of obstacles, service experiences can strengthen our resilience, teaching us valuable lessons about perseverance and the power of a positive impact.

Encourages gratitude

Service provides a perspective that can profoundly shift our outlook on life, cultivating a deep gratitude for what we have. By engaging with others whose circumstances may differ vastly from ours, we better understand our privileges and blessings. This awareness can transform our approach to challenges, encouraging a focus on gratitude over dissatisfaction.

Promotes Personal Reflection and Growth

Service is often a mirror, reflecting to us our values, judgments, and biases. It challenges us to question and reflect upon our beliefs and behaviors, promoting personal growth. This reflective process can lead to a more authentic life aligned with our deepest values and convictions.

Cultivates a Sense of Purpose

Perhaps most significantly, service to others can anchor us to a sense of purpose. Service offers a clear path to meaning in a world where many feel adrift and unsure of their place or contribution. It reassures us that our actions can have a positive impact, that our lives have significance beyond our immediate concerns, and that we are part of a larger narrative of care and connection.

Enhances Skills and Knowledge

Service also offers practical benefits, including developing new skills and knowledge. Whether learning to communicate more effectively, manage projects, or understand specific social issues, serving others can enhance our professional and personal competencies, making us more well-rounded and capable.

In essence, service is a profound path to personal growth, offering lessons and experiences that enrich our lives in countless ways. It challenges us to look beyond ourselves, to connect with others in meaningful ways, and to contribute to the world with empathy, compassion, and purpose. Through service, we not only impact the lives of others but also embark on a journey of self-discovery and development, finding fulfillment in the act of giving and growing in the process.

This examination of resilience, personal development, and the transformational potential of accepting life's obstacles concludes with the observation that the path to fulfillment and self-improvement is deeply individualized and shared by all. Through the chapters on discovering inner brilliance, nurturing authenticity, and cultivating gratitude, among others, we've delved into the essence of living a life marked by purpose, empathy, and a commitment to growth.

This book has underscored the importance of looking inward to find strength and outward to engage with the world in meaningful ways.

It's shown us that resilience isn't about avoiding challenges but about facing them with courage, learning from them, and emerging stronger. We've seen how acts of kindness and service benefit others and enrich our lives, fostering a sense of connection and community.

At the heart of this journey is the understanding that personal growth is a continuous process shaped by our experiences, choices, and the relationships we cultivate. It's a path marked by moments of joy, periods of struggle, and the countless small decisions that steer us toward becoming more compassionate, resilient, and fulfilled individuals.

Let us take the knowledge acquired, the lessons learned, and the attitude of thankfulness and service permeating these pages as we finish this chapter. Let us embrace life's challenges and changes not as obstacles but as opportunities for growth, leading with love, serving with purpose, and continually seeking to understand ourselves and the world around us more deeply.

In this journey of personal growth and development, remember that each step, no matter how small, moves us closer to the light of our inner brilliance, guiding us toward a life filled with purpose, connection, and joy.